THE MUSICAL CHILD

THE
MUSICAL
CHILD

USING THE POWER OF MUSIC TO
RAISE CHILDREN WHO ARE HAPPY,
HEALTHY, AND WHOLE

JOAN KOENIG

HOUGHTON MIFFLIN HARCOURT
BOSTON   NEW YORK   2021

For information about permission to reproduce selections from this book,
write to trade.permissions@hmhco.com or to Permissions,
Houghton Mifflin Harcourt Publishing Company, 3 Park Avenue,
19th Floor, New York, New York 10016.

hmhbooks.com

Library of Congress Cataloging-in-Publication Data
Names: Koenig, Joan, author.
Title: The musical child : using the power of music to raise children who
are happy, healthy, and whole / Joan Koenig.
Description: Boston : Houghton Mifflin Harcourt, 2021. |
Includes bibliographical references and index.
Identifiers: LCCN 2020050865 (print) | LCCN 2020050866 (ebook) |
ISBN 9781328612960 (hardcover) | ISBN 9780358449874 |
ISBN 9780358450269 | ISBN 9781328613035 (ebook)
Subjects: LCSH: Music and children. | Child development.
Classification: LCC ML83 .K64 2021 (print) | LCC ML83 (ebook) |
DDC 780.71—dc23
LC record available at https://lccn.loc.gov/2020050865
LC ebook record available at https://lccn.loc.gov/2020050866

Book design by Kelly Dubeau Smydra
Illustrations by Julie Menuet Le Her
Musical scores by Joan Koenig & Aurélien Parent Koenig

Infographic on page 19 is from *Communicative Musicality: Exploring the
Basis of Human Companionship*, edited by Stephen Malloch and
Colwyn Trevarthen. Copyright © 2009 by Oxford University Press.
Reproduced with permission of OUP through PLSclear.

Printed in the United States of America

1 2021
4500826423

To all the children with whom I have had the joy of sharing music;

to my children, Aurélien and Elsa,

and their partners, Tomas and Sercan;

and to the coming generation.

Oh, the places you'll go!

— DR. SEUSS

CONTENTS

Author's Note

The names of the children, parents, and teachers have been changed, with the exception of those who requested their first names appear in the book.

INTRODUCTION

THERE ARE FEW UNIVERSALS IN THIS WORLD, but among them are our love for our children and our love of music. When we cradle baby in our arms, soothing her with song, we are channelling the emotional power of music. We do so instinctively, just as our ancestors did. Music can be a powerful parental ally during the challenging child-rearing years. All parents and educators can access this natural source of pleasure, comfort, and stimulation, because we are a musical species.

To successfully prepare our children for life in the twenty-first century, we will need to nurture qualities such as curiosity, imagination, intuition, empathy, creative entrepreneurship, and most of all resilience. Musical practice in early childhood develops all of the above and more. Research has shown that musical practice in early childhood is beneficial not only for mental acuity but for social and emotional development as well. Music is not just a hobby, a pleasant pastime; it is an integral part of what makes us happy, healthy, and whole. Indeed, if we want to do one thing to help our children develop into emotionally, socially, intellectually, and creatively competent human beings, we should start the musical conversation — the earlier the better.

Children need music in their lives, but not for putative cognitive gains. Children need to make music together because this is how they learn to become a "we," with the challenges *and* the deep satisfaction this involves. Today, more than ever, children need to experience the exhilaration of a collective effort. Music acts as a magnet for this — it always has.

Humans were making music together long before the first note was written on the first staff, but the practice has largely disappeared from our daily lives. Music has never been so readily available on so many platforms, and yet we are several generations into the false belief that musicking — my preferred term for musical practice — requires arduous training.* In highly developed societies where music is instantly available on multiple devices, I see less and less spontaneous musicking in homes. Rather than singing and dancing with them, we send our children to music class. This is as developmentally absurd as not speaking with your child and sending her to weekly language lessons in her native tongue.

There is an easy and natural way to include the wonders of music in children's lives. I know, because I have spent most of my life doing it.

My own musical journey began in the basement of my family home. My parents were not musical; we did not have season tickets to the Philharmonic, nor did my parents play records on the stereo. Although my mother had no formal musical training, she believed strongly in the virtues of music. One of her certitudes was that every home should have a piano, so when I was four years old, a piano took up residence in our family room. I remember sitting down to "play," touching the keys and experimenting with the sounds they made. I found monsters in the bass notes and fairies fluttering in

---

* The gerund "musicking" comes from the German noun *Musik*. A gerund is a verb form that also functions as a noun; in English, the added *-ing* ending magically transforms otherwise static words like *cook, play,* and *music* into action. The musicologist Christopher Small (1927–2011) proposed that the word "musicking" enter the English dictionary and include all aspects of music making, including dance.

the highest notes. These musical experiments were a continual source of pleasure and learning. My piano was my favorite toy — and my creative accomplice.

As with many American homes of that era, the radio was very much a part of our lives. One of my father's favorite radio hits was "Que Sera, Sera," sung by Doris Day. I remember thinking that perhaps my piano could produce this song, though I wasn't sure how. Like most children who have access to a keyboard, I began experimenting. Finding the first notes was easy, but then I got stuck where the notes became nonconsecutive. I spent hours negotiating these jumps until I finally figured it out. There it was, "Que Sera, Sera." It felt as though I had broken the code. If I could find the beginning of this song through trial and error, I could find the entire song, and then I could find any song. Finding melodies like this invariably leads to more playing around — or what I like to call musical scribbling — and this leads to improvisation. Today, science confirms the positive impact that creative experimentation has on young minds. It is a door that can easily open in early childhood and remain open for life. Although I am a classical musician, many of my most thrilling performing experiences have involved improvisation. I know that my ability to improvise stems from these first experiments in early childhood.

My childhood and adolescence were filled with music. I began formal piano lessons at the age of five, and when I was nine years old, I asked if I could take up the flute as well, because I wanted to play in a band or an orchestra. Music programs with instrumental training were still part of the public school curriculum in those prehistoric times. A few years and many hours of practicing later, I auditioned for a local youth orchestra made up of young musicians from the greater Seattle area. Members of the orchestra were encouraged to attend a high-level summer camp offering chamber music and orchestral training. It may have been this first musical summer camp that sealed the deal. I loved playing in an orchestra, and I loved living and breathing music. I began seriously practicing the flute after that summer. I subsequently obtained scholarships to the Interlochen Arts Camp and the Aspen Music Festival. I entered competitions and won awards, performance opportunities, and, finally, entrance to the Juilliard School in 1977.

In 1981, upon graduation from Juilliard, I moved to Paris. Just as aspiring chefs come to France for the culinary traditions, flutists come for the incomparable French school of flute playing. I loved Paris, and I loved learning a second language. Little did I know that I would never leave. Instead, I embarked on a performing career, got married, had children, created a music school, and then a musical preschool.

L'École Koenig opened its doors in 1986 and grew steadily both in size and in scope. Twenty-two years later, in 2008, I decided to take my program a step further. I had witnessed young children's extraordinary musical ability in weekly music classes; I needed to see what would happen if children lived and learned in music every day. So with the help of my courageous staff, we opened a trilingual preschool where the children speak French, English — and music.

At our musical preschool, children are encouraged to improvise songs and stories, which they do readily because music is one of the languages that they are learning. Music is an integral part of all learning in our classrooms; even reading and writing are taught with music and movement. And although the preschool program at L'École Koenig is still relatively young, we are obtaining extraordinary results.

Music can accelerate learning and helps imprint knowledge and experience into lifelong memory. We see children learning their letter sounds instantly by singing and dancing their phonetic alphabet song. Multiplication tables are memorized in a single morning when the children rap and groove with them. More importantly, we observe children of more than twenty different nationalities joyfully singing and dancing together: learning and communicating through their one common language, music.

Not long after opening the musical preschool at L'École Koenig, I also began immersing myself in the world of science — particularly neuroscience. What I found was thrilling and transformative. An exciting, and growing, body of research is illuminating the science behind the effects our staff and I were seeing in our young students — underscoring the extraordinary benefits of musical practice in early childhood.

In 2014 I was invited to be a fellow at the Salzburg Global Seminar, and an entirely new chapter in my life began. Salzburg Global organizes conferences on matters of global importance — bringing together people from all over the world to reflect, learn from one another, and bring about change. This conference was titled "The Neuroscience of Art," and of the forty participants, half were artists and half were scientists. I like to say that at that time, I didn't know my hippocampus from my amygdala. But the resulting collaborations with neuroscientists from all over the world have allowed me to corroborate, deepen, and strengthen my understanding of the human mind and the vital place that music occupies in our human construction. I had the empirical evidence before; now I understood the supporting science as well.

Today we have more than thirty years of research into the musical practice and the brain, showing clearly that music helps us develop vital physical coordination, fine-tunes our speech and auditory systems, and reinforces memory. Most importantly, musical practice lifts us out of ourselves into an intuitive, cooperative, and deeply satisfying relationship with others.

One of the most beautiful illustrations of these qualities in vivo is the orchestra. The orchestra can serve as a model for collective creation, even when it doesn't involve musical instruments. Many of our hard-earned societal victories are in danger today, and trust in government is low the world over. We need an inspiring model like the orchestra more than ever because the systems that we rely upon are crumbling. The orchestral model is not about accumulating individual capital gains or securing power; the orchestra's raison d'être is the creation of beauty by combining our strengths and talent.

Meaningful life in the twenty-first century will involve working in groups to find creative solutions to global challenges — among them climate change and the massive population movements this will inevitably cause. The specter of species extinction calls for cool and creative minds to study the facts and find sustainable solutions. This will demand innovation and an ability to boldly and creatively identify and connect what might strike others as random dots.

Musical practice builds the foundation for creative thinking, especially when it occurs in early childhood. Making the dots on a musical score come to life with your instrument engages your mind, body, and soul. Improvising is an equally complex process, and they both require countless physical, cognitive, and intuitive connections. Playing with absolute precision with others adds yet another layer of complexity — and pleasure.

Learning and working together as an orchestra can prepare us for many other endeavors. Life-changing innovations are rarely the work of one person. They involve sharing knowledge, increasingly from the far corners of the planet, arguing, comparing, fearlessly experimenting, and constantly remaining eager, open, and receptive to new ideas.

The orchestra is a vital concept and a model, and one that needn't be intimidating. Orchestral play can take place anywhere, with any subject, and — as you will see — the orchestra can be made up of very small people, not just classically trained adults. There is no need to wait for children to have the motor skills to play the violin before offering them an orchestral experience.

Most musical programs neglect the opportunity for pre-instrumental musical practice, which means we are missing the ideal moment to develop aural expertise. Musicking at an early age is not simply about developing one's natural musical ability; it is also about learning to coexist with other people at an age at which "me" generally prevails. Before even learning an instrument, our children can learn to work together as an orchestra does: listening carefully, making adjustments, working toward something much bigger than the sum of its parts.

This book will explain the profound effect music can have on children's developing minds and bodies, the more than thirty years of scientific research on this subject that has not yet trickled down into our homes and schools. My goal is to share this research with you alongside stories and examples of real children and their musical journeys. I also will guide you through music and movement games that you can enjoy with the child in your own life, beginning in infancy. None of these games require previous musical training; indeed, after one or two of them, you will see how easy it is to tap into your own natural musicality, even if you are convinced that you have none.

Since this is a book about music, you are probably going to want to hear the music described in these pages. This book is designed for you to be able to hear the music of each proposed activity instantly, via QR (Quick Response) codes. Each chapter has a QR code that you can scan with your phone.

There are multiple apps available for QR code scanning on smartphones, and many are free of charge. When you scan the QR image, you will be automatically directed to the website www.joankoenig .com where all the original music is available. You can of course just go directly to the website. If you are a musician, simple scores to the music mentioned are in the appendix.

Enjoy!

At its heart, the goal of this book is simple: to help you and your child embark on a fun-filled creative musical journey together and reap the benefits throughout both your lifetimes. In the process, you will be preparing yourselves to take your places in the Orchestra of Humankind.

THE MUSICAL CHILD

1 YEAR ONE
The First Duet

SCAN ME

I'S A CRISP OCTOBER MORNING IN PARIS, AND AT L'École Koenig, excitement is in the air: the fourth Baby Musicking class of the school year is about to begin. Parents and teachers alike are eagerly anticipating another chance to experience the immediate and joyful reactions of these tiny infants, who range in age from three to twelve months.

Our school has three separate locations, all within a five-hundred-meter area of Paris's 15th arrondissement. The Baby Musicking room, which is located next door to our main conservatory and kindergarten campus, is a brightly colored living room–sized space, with thick blue carpeting for comfortable rolling around—for both the babies and the adults. There is one piano for our pianist, and one piano stripped of its decorative outer shell: a sort of naked version of the instrument, which we denuded by unhooking the wooden cover above the keyboard that hid the piano hammers, and by removing the cover below the keyboard that hid the lowest and longest strings. This left the keys, strings, and hammers exposed for children to explore, which they do tirelessly. A big conga drum is lying on the floor for baby exploration, along with a small harp and several xylophones.

It takes a few minutes for everyone to exchange greetings, remove their shoes and coats. Soon, parents and caretakers are seated on the floor in a "magic circle," grinning and waiting for the music to begin. After only a few classes, we also sense the babies' eager anticipation; seated on the adults' laps, they become silent and still, clearly waiting. As soon as their teacher Marion counts down from five, and the music begins, the babies start waving their arms, swaying back and forth and vocalizing, which is to say, loudly and happily squawking.

After the "Bonjour/Good Morning" song, Marion launches into a game of rhythmic call-and-response that includes clapping and stomping. The youngest babies try their best to respond: we see them rocking, but their little hands and feet are not yet cooperating.

Next we begin our unique method of calling roll. Each baby has a musical name — a short fragment of music composed to reflect the child's personality and to match the number of syllables in their name. The parents and caretakers join in, greeting each child by singing their musical name, enthusiastically moving in time with the music. An air of unity and joy fills the room.

When eight-month-old Maximilian hears his musical name, a fragment of a salsa rhythm, he is initially silent and motionless, as if making sure that this is indeed *his* music. And then he's off, swaying with delight, waving his arms and loudly vocalizing. We sing his name several times as he revels in the group's attention.

Baby's Musical Name

Would you like to make a melody out of your baby's name? I suggest that you try the following exercise. You might just be thrilled by the results.

Take the number of syllables in baby's name and make a melody. Let's take the name Gabrielle. You can sing the three syllables moving up, just like Do-Re-Mi,

or descending, Mi-Re-Do.

You don't have to start on a specific pitch; just start somewhere that feels comfortable for your voice. No need to feel self-conscious about this. Think of your favorite folk, rock, or R&B songs: the singers don't just sing the notes, they inhabit them. You can also use the beginning of a song you know and just repeat her name to fit the melody. For example, "Amazing Grace" becomes:

Or "Jingle Bells," with its easy-to-retain short-short-long rhythm, is an easy fit for three-syllable names:

Take your baby in your arms and lift or bend according to the rising or falling melodic movement of your song. Now play around: speed up, slow down; use a high voice or a deep, throaty voice. If you have chosen "Jingle Bells," dance to the rhythm with corresponding movements: short-short-long, short-short-long.

Pay attention to which aspects your baby likes best — and stick with what works.

Within a few weeks, you will notice that this song — your baby's very own musical name — will bring on a smile, and also calm your baby when she is distressed. Why? Because this is *her* song. This is a little tiny masterpiece that you have created for her. She recognizes your loving intention, as well as the shape of the melody and the feel of the rhythm. The song is your personal duet: an act of love and connection that she will participate in long before she can actually sing along or move with you.

One morning, not much later in the school year, Max's mother placed the tambourine she had been using on the floor near Max's foot. As our pianist improvised an especially rock-and-roll piece of music, Max inadvertently hit the tambourine with his foot. Seeming both surprised and pleased to have made the sound, he did what every baby does when experiencing something new: he tried it again.

Then he grabbed the tambourine with both hands and began shaking it back and forth. When I moved closer to him with my drum and began to play along with him, Max grew still.

He was staring intently at me, and I could almost see the cogs turning in his little head. He tested me several times, shaking the tambourine once, twice, three times. I would answer with the same number of beats on my drum. Our pianist was following along closely, playing in time with both of us, adding a harmonic layer of resonant chords. Suddenly this spontaneous little exchange was beginning to sound like something more.

We can scarcely imagine what this might feel like to an eight-month-old child, to hear his tentative tambourine-tapping morph into a symphonic work that he appears to be conducting. Max had stopped smiling and now was concentrating his gaze on me, barely moving. Then he began vocalizing, oohing and aahing excitedly. I answered his vocalizations, but he was taking the lead, the conductor directing our nonverbal conversation.

Finally, Max put the small tambourine in his mouth, which was such classic eight-month-old behavior that everyone in the classroom had to laugh. Max signaled that our conversation was over by dropping the tambourine and reaching up to his mother, who proudly smothered him with kisses as the room erupted in applause.

The following week, as we sat down for class again, it was evident that Max not only remembered the game but also wanted to relive the experience. He smiled at me and began tapping his tambourine and vocalizing as soon as his mother settled onto the carpet with him. Once again, this time with certainty, Maximilian was showing us that he was ready to engage in what I call "the first duet."

LOOK WHO'S TALKING . . .

The musical child's journey begins in the first year of life. So much is happening in baby's brain and body during this first year, and research has shown that music is a powerful means of communication at this stage of life. Stimulating a child's innate musicality sets the stage for healthy cognitive, emotional, and physical development, and above all, self-confidence.

To be sure, there have been far too many claims made about music making your child smarter. Even if this could be proven, moreover, it isn't the primary reason to expose the youngest children to music. Your baby needs a music-infused exchange — the first duet — to reassure herself that she is not alone and, therefore, not in danger. Every sound, every gesture that elicits a response from you confirms in her mind that she exists, that she is safe, and that you are there for her. Even the most basic musical exchanges develop baby's sense of security — the cornerstone of self-confidence, which in turn sets the stage for learning and happiness.

Your baby's brain development mirrors the way the human brain evolved over the millennia — from the bottom up. At the base of the brain, sitting on top of the spinal cord, is a set of structures known collectively as the limbic system, home to our emotional, sensory, and memory centers. Inside the limbic system is the amygdala, one of the key centers for emotional processing Next to the amygdala is the hippocampus, one of our memory processing centers. These two have a veritable communication hotline in place. Both the hippocampus and the amygdala play a crucial role in processing emotional aspects of memories. Music processing strongly engages this highly emotional and reactive part of the brain.

At the front of the brain sits the prefrontal cortex, the seat of analysis, judgment, and executive function, the set of cognitive processes, from short-term memory to the sorting of information, that underlie self-awareness, emotional regulation, planning, and problem solving. The only difficulty for baby, and for you, is that this part of the brain is not even close to fully developed at birth. As an adult, you can manage fear or sadness or confusion with reason and through the benefit of experience. This is your executive function stepping in, lending a rational helping hand. Baby simply does not have this equipment; she is raw sensation and emotion. Her prefrontal cortex, where rationality lives, won't develop fully until late adolescence or early adulthood.

Research dating from as far back as 1980 determined that a fetus's sense of hearing is already functioning in the third trimester in utero. Newborns prefer their mother's voice at birth, clearly demonstrating that they recognize this voice from *before* birth. With fully functioning hearing and a ripe and ready limbic system, baby is biologically prepared to experience music from day one. The effect can be powerful, providing the comfort and reassurance that underlie her emotional stability and well-being. Music affects babies intensely because it engages proportionally more parts of their brain at this stage of their development. Every warm moment of connection is processed in the limbic system, and even if these experiences can't be recalled, they become a part of who we are. Think of the firm foundation of well-being that we can provide by singing and engaging with our babies.

Human beings are naturally sensitive and responsive to melody and rhythm. Almost without exception, babies — all humans, in fact — have a spontaneous physical and emotional reaction to music. You probably have a favorite song, and most likely find yourself tapping your toes in time or becoming emotional upon hearing a memorable piece of music from your past. This is clear and simple proof that you are sensitive to music, that you are musical, even if you never think of yourself that way. And that's all you need to engage with your baby in this elemental musical way.

What are your favorite pieces of music? Whatever the answer, now is the time to share them with your baby. I met a new father recently who had a child late in life. Daniel grew up during the musically prolific 1970s. He told me how he had been dutifully putting on special baby music for his daughter, and hating every minute of it. I asked him what music he loved, and he immediately started gushing about the Stones, the Beatles, ABBA, and Dolly Parton. I laughed and told him to throw away the baby albums, put on Dolly, pick up Patsy, and dance! This shared joy is like a superfood for the mind, the body, and the heart — and not just for baby!

You do not need professional training to make music with your child. Even if you think you sing off-key, or believe you have two left feet, your baby wants to sing and dance with you. This first duet will bring your child happiness and contribute to her healthy development. I will suggest simple techniques, and the science underlying them, so that you can share musical experiences with your child from the moment she's born. The potential pleasures and benefits to both you and your child are boundless.

What can we learn from Maximilian's duet about an eight-month-old infant's need to communicate? When I joined in with Max, we were engaging in a musical conversation. For an eight-month-old baby, a conversation needs no words, but it does require your full attention. In this case, Max was initiating our interaction and taking the lead. This is an example of the moment when a baby realizes that he can provoke a response from another human being through his voice or actions. Max was learning that he could, in a sense, ask me a question and that I would respond.

Max and I were creating a narrative together. There were no words, but there was meaning. This is an important part of the first duet — the essential dialogue that every baby seeks. And it is enhanced by music. In fact, decades of research suggest that babies prefer music to speech.

Your First Duet

You may doubt your musical ability, but you cannot doubt your ability to speak. The first duet does not have to include musical instruments. All you need are your voice, your imagination, and your body. This simple exercise will get you started.

Sit down and place your baby face-up on your thighs, with her head on your knees, her feet touching your stomach. You can sing or whisper just about anything — even made-up nonsense words — as long as you are not afraid to modulate your voice. Take her feet or hands (or, ideally, one of each) and gently move them in sync to your words or your song. We know that babies prefer song to speech, so this is the moment to let go of any fear of singing. Keep constant eye contact with your baby. Pretend you are a mime, and use every facial expression you can. Don't be afraid to be silly; open your mouth and stick out your tongue. Your baby will probably do the same!

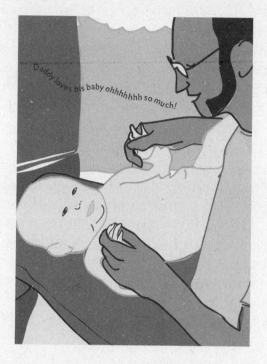

You look so lovely in your beautiful blue pajamas!
Daddy loves his baby ohhhhhhh so much!
Let's make some pancakes, pancakes, pancakes...

Remember that repetition is necessary for baby because it develops her ability to predict what will come next — and when it does, she is happily reassured. This is one of the principal ways that babies learn. Listen very closely to your baby's tiny sounds and try to answer with something that keeps the conversation going. Repeat the sounds that baby makes, and perhaps add on, much like you might in an adult conversation: "Oh, really? I had no idea!"

Be sure to also pay attention to your baby's facial expressions and movements. You can imitate them, and then try adding something new, like a raised eyebrow. Try moving your mouth in a funny way and accompanying the movement with a "pop" sound. Your baby will surely begin to imitate these facial expressions, which is a crucial part of her development. (Imitation is one of the first steps on baby's path to absorbing the codes of her culture. The youngest baby imitation on record was a newborn: she stuck out her little tongue in imitation forty-two minutes after birth.) Most importantly, if your baby smiles or gurgles, repeat whatever you are doing; she is telling you that she likes this and wants to hear it again.

As your baby grows, these conversations often become like comedy routines. You might ask a question during mealtime, only to have your child answer with a litany that sounds like a song in a foreign language. Observing the birth of language in a baby is extraordinary; no wonder scientists have been trying to understand the musicality of this uniquely human ability for decades.

When Max and I took turns banging on our drums and "oohing" and "aahing," we were having what linguists call a "proto-conversation." A proto-conversation consists of sounds, gestures, and meaning before the onset of language in a child. The musical conversation I shared with Max is a vibrant example of this duet. I am a professional musician, but when I had my first child, my classical music training was the furthest thing from my mind. Singing with my baby was instinctive. My own mother sang a great deal in my early childhood. She had no musical training, but if she had any insecurity about her musicality, she never let it get in the way. We are a musical species; musicking takes place all over the world, in most cases without professional training.

The first duet is a prelude to language and well-being, but how does this work exactly? The research on infant language acquisition and musicality began more than sixty years ago, long before neuroscience, fMRI (functional magnetic resonance imaging) scanners, and our modern fascination with the mind-body connection. We are going to look at the extraordinary findings of a group of researchers at Harvard in the 1960s — findings that redefined our understanding of the critical developments during the first years of life. Babies are listening and learning even before they are born. They are learning to speak long before they delight us with their first words, and the key to all of this learning lies in human interaction, or the first duet.

THE BABY WHISPERERS

In 1967 the psychologists Jerome Bruner and George A. Miller set up the Harvard Center for Cognitive Studies. Psychological research was stagnating in 1956 when Miller, a professor at Harvard, delivered a paper titled "The Magical Number Seven, Plus or Minus Two." The paper set off an explosion of research into how memory works. Miller was the quintessential "out of the box" thinker. To create the protocol for his evaluation of short-term memory, he borrowed a model from the virtually unknown field of computer coding — in 1956! Miller revolutionized the world of psychology by demonstrating that although the mind is invisible, it can be tested.

Jerome Bruner was also a brilliant iconoclast who was constantly reinventing himself. During his seventy-year academic career he constantly moved from one field to another, bringing new and notable contributions in areas as diverse as music, education, physics, literature, and the law. In his own words, the basis of his work was the study of cognition, or what he called "the great question of how you know anything." Bruner and Miller are considered the instigators of what would become known as the cognitive revolution. Their team included some of the finest minds in the field at the time: Colwyn Trevarthen, T. Berry Brazelton, Edward Tronick, and Noam Chomsky.

Bruner wanted to investigate nothing less than the foundations of language — infant modes of communication beginning at birth.

His team began to film and study interactions between preverbal babies and their mothers. One of the team members, Colwyn Trevarthen, was using a filming technique that could film at sixty-four frames per second, almost three times the standard twenty-four fps. This new technique would provide high-quality slow-motion footage that allowed the team to detect and study the baby's slightest gestures and vocalizations.

Trevarthen's filming technique uncovered something incredible. Not only did the researchers find that babies were cognizant of their caretakers and interacting with them, but also they observed that babies were often taking the lead — *initiating* the proto-conversation.

The prevailing language theory at the time was the work of Noam Chomsky, who believed that children have an innate ability to learn language because they are born with a *language acquisition device* (LAD). Bruner disagreed and cheekily coined a term for his own theory: *language acquisition support system* (LASS). He concluded that children learn to speak not from innate hardwiring but rather through human interaction. Colwyn Trevarthen was in agreement, and further qualified infant language acquisition as a "turn-taking structure of conversation that develops through games and nonverbal communication long before the onset of actual words." The entire brilliant team agreed on the fact that babies seek communication, beginning at birth, and that this need must be met for healthy development.

Bruner did not just coin the memorable term for his new theory of language learning; he also was the first to give a name to the specific way adults speak to babies. He called it *child-directed speech*.

MOTHERESE

There is a specific form of child-directed speech that parents use with their children in all cultures and languages, usually referred to as Motherese or Parentese. The musical, vocal, and imitation elements that constitute Motherese are all part of the first duet. They are inherently musical, and breathe life into the child's emotional, cognitive, and physical development.

We are all fluent in Motherese; certain unconscious behaviors appear to surface when we are in the company of an infant. We address the baby in a lilting musical manner, typically without even thinking about it. It might sound something like "Oohh my sweeeeet beauuuuuuutiful baaaaaby!" And what does baby do? She engages immediately, emotionally, vocally, and physically. Not only does she engage, but also she will prompt you if you are not keeping up your end of the conversation.

The term "Motherese" first appeared in a 1975 doctoral dissertation by Elissa Newport, a student at the University of Pennsylvania. The author was studying the speech women used with their daughters, but she also acknowledged the role of fathers and caretakers in infant language acquisition. In an article in the *New York Times Magazine* in 1994 (written under the pseudonym "Motherese"), she defended her choice of this gender-specific term. "Newer terms take into account that fathers and others influence the child's language," she wrote. "I've heard 'caretaker talk' and 'child-directed speech,' but no single word is as effective as Motherese."

There may be an evolutionary reason why adult humans speak to their infants in the particular way that Newport, and Bruner before her, described. Motherese allows mothers to attend to their very dependent infants in a manner that is emotionally satisfying and therefore pleasurable for both parties. This can actually be considered, in the Darwinian sense, necessary for the survival of the species, given that a newborn's survival is dependent entirely on her parents or caretakers, and that helpless babies are going to need a great deal of attention for a very long time. One researcher thinks that this win-win emotional duet is actually necessary for the survival of both child *and* parent.

How did Motherese develop? Why are human babies so very helpless when compared to other mammals? About 6 million years ago, when our ancestors began the slow process of moving from all fours to an upright position, the body had to evolve. Some of the most significant changes involved the female body and concerned gestation and childbirth. The birth canal was becoming shorter and smaller at the same time that the human brain was becoming larger. Very gradually, over millennia, the gestation period decreased, resulting in a smaller, less mature baby — with a smaller head. The result of all of these extraordinary evolutionary events is that at birth, human babies are the most helpless newborn mammals on earth. To achieve the level of independence of a newborn chimpanzee, our babies would need a gestation period of twenty-one months and would weigh roughly twenty-five pounds at birth.

Therefore, from about 1.6 million years ago, the human baby was born essentially premature in terms of neurological development, and unable to survive on its own. These helpless babies required 24/7 care, yet their mothers also needed to take care of hearth and home. Among the difficulties faced by these early working mothers was that their babies, unlike other mammals, were not born with the ability to hold on to their mother's neck or waist while she worked. They could not even sit up on their own for the first six months or so. When a mother needed to prepare a meal, she had to set the baby down, and her attention would be divided between her chore and her baby. She could, however, sing and coo, thus engaging her baby with sound, and keeping the baby "with" her via their vocal exchange.

The universality of Motherese across cultures lends credibility to this theory. The fact that an infant's hearing is almost fully developed at birth means that even if she does not see her mother, she will hear her and respond, even at a distance, thus freeing her mother to carry on with other chores. The musical dialogue maintains the constant communication necessary to guarantee that baby is safe while allowing mom the freedom to take care of dinner, which, of course, contributes to everyone's survival. Motherese has become part of our instinctive behavior, one of our *sapiens*-specific practices.

THE MOTHER OF ALL DISCOURSE

Like the Harvard team, many scientists now consider Motherese to be one of the primal ingredients of social intercourse: the first form of communication for any human. Human babies need communication to survive, and they demonstrate a consistent cross-cultural preference for song over speech.

The disastrous effect on children of the lack of human communication was documented in the tragically impoverished orphanages that were exposed in the 1990s in Romania after the death of the president and dictator Nicolae Ceausescu. In one such case, a British NGO (nongovernmental organization) called the White Rose Initiative intervened in an orphanage in Bucharest with eighty children and two caretakers. Children were left strapped to their beds with minimal human contact. The children could not speak, and were physically, emotionally, and cognitively impaired. They did not engage with one another because they did not know how. They had no one to imitate, no one from whom they could learn.

Even in this extreme situation, however, the interventions provided by the NGO — playing with the children, speaking with them, engaging them physically and emotionally — brought about immediate positive results. One of the participants, Sophie Webb, said that it was as if those tiny untapped brains were simply "waiting for someone to turn on the electricity."

Sadly, in most cases these interventions occurred too late for these children to develop into independent adults; their first, vital years of human interaction had been lost, and their brains and bodies would never fully recover. Infant neglect is hard to study for obvious reasons — but one of the psychologists associated with the Harvard center managed to document the dramatic effect of just a few moments of neglect on an otherwise healthy baby.

Edward Tronick is a developmental psychologist and specialist in early childhood communication. In 1975 Tronick made a video that is now referred to as the "still face" experiment. Videos did not "go viral" in 1975, but if they had, this one would certainly have made it to the top of the YouTube charts. In the video, a young mother and her eleven-month-old daughter engage in a delightful nonverbal exchange, or proto-conversation. The baby is in a highchair, and the mother is leaning in toward her, touching her hands and cooing, almost singing. The baby points at something, knowing that her mother will look in that direction, and she does. They are "matching their intentions," according to Tronick.

Then, as the protocol requires, the mother turns away. When she turns back to the baby, her face bears a blank, neutral expression. She is no longer engaging. The baby tries the "ah" greeting and gets no response. She valiantly employs her entire skill set; she claps, smiles, and points, finally putting both hands up in the air as if to say, "What is going on here?" Then she claps her hands and yells. She ends up turning away, wailing, and even slumping down in her highchair. When the mother abandons the "still face" and comes back, the baby immediately relaxes, and they take up their musical proto-conversation as if nothing had happened.

Like Bruner and Trevarthen, Tronick believes that this initial conversation is how infants create what he called "meaning, emotional connections, movements, and representations about themselves in relation to the world." This is the foundation of the infant's future relationship with everyone and everything around her.

Much of Tronick's subsequent research involves examining what happens when this duet does *not* take place. The answer is painfully clear: the child's development suffers. Thankfully the little girl in the film was not in a Romanian orphanage; she had to endure her mother's absence for only a few moments. There were no permanent scars.

If you are reading this book, it is unlikely that you are ignoring your baby — but still, I cannot emphasize enough how important this first duet is to your child's development. Babies need oral communication. Their engagement is heightened when this communication involves song. Their highly developed auditory system is ripe and ready for precisely this even before day one. Infants need constant human contact, first to reassure them that they are not alone, and second, to learn how to become people themselves.

Imagine the field of neonatal research at the time. The learning curve was vertiginous. Only a few years prior, babies were considered blank slates with no emotional life. Operations were performed with no anesthesia because infants were thought to have no feelings or memory capacity.

In the past fifty years, thankfully, developmental stages in early childhood have been redefined. The cursor indicating the onset of feelings, conscience, and pain has been moving steadily backwards toward birth. Colwyn Trevarthen was, and remains, a major protagonist in this movement.

From his early experience with Bruner at the Harvard Center for Cognitive Studies, Trevarthen went on to became a professor of child psychology and psychobiology at the University of Edinburgh in Scotland. He would devote his life to infant communication — the first duet. He confided in me that once babies acquire language, he loses interest.

In his late eighties at the time of our conversation, Trevarthen spent a lifetime leaning over cribs and observing neonate behavior — more than fifty years and counting. Trevarthen explains that when his first child was born, he decided that he would probably learn more by studying human babies than baboon brains, so he changed his field of research from primates to child psychology.

In 1996 Trevarthen was operating his own lab at the University of Edinburg, filming, studying, and comparing baby-and-mother exchanges from all over the world. In another lab nearby, Stephen Malloch, a music and physics student at the university, was hard at work devising a means of measuring subtle acoustic variations in music. He was trying to make the variations visible to the naked eye on a graph. Only a day after Malloch had presented his spectrograph (or sound graphic) to his music teacher, Professor Nigel Osborn, Trevarthen happened to complain to Osborn that he could really use a more sophisticated means of analyzing tiny baby voices. Introductions were swiftly made, and Trevarthen and Malloch began a collaboration that would result in a seminal body of work in the field of infant musicality and communication.

Trevarthen began by giving Malloch the film he had made of an exchange between four-month-old Laura and her mother. Malloch described taking it "upstairs to a dark, windowless room high up in the Edinburg University Psychology Department" to begin watching the film, enjoying the lilting musical quality of the mother's voice. Suddenly he realized that he had started tapping his foot. "I replayed the tape, and again, I could sense a distinct rhythmicity and melodious give-and-take to the gentle prompting of Laura's mother and the pitched vocal replies from Laura." The experience was pivotal for Malloch, and soon the words *communicative musicality* came to him to describe the scope and importance of what he had observed.

By analyzing the spectrograph recordings, Malloch and Trevarthen began to realize that the mother-baby exchange they were observing strongly resembled a musical composition. In musical terms, there was an *introduction* (the main melodic theme is introduced), a *development* (the theme is elaborated), a *climax* (the moment of highest musical tension), and finally the release and a *coda* (a new motif leading to the end of the piece). As with music, the baby's last utterance was descending and held just a bit longer than the previous sounds. Composers and musicians call this a *fermata:* the practice of remaining on the note much longer than the actual rhythmic value, indicating a pause or an ending. All of this took place in a twenty-seven-second conversation between little Laura and her mother.

Trevarthen and Malloch were pioneers. In the decades following their first observations, research into the role of vocal and musical exchanges in early infancy accelerated — as did investigation into the mysterious links between music, language, and emotion. The advent of neuroscience, and our ability to observe a functioning brain, can actually show us what is going on in that little baby brain — whether baby is cooing softly or screeching with frustration. The prominent role of music as a means of soothing or stimulating is no longer just an impression; as of this writing, we have more than

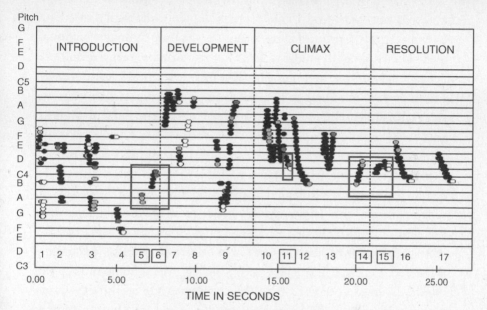

INTRODUCTION	DEVELOPMENT	CLIMAX	RESOLUTION
1 Come on	7 Oh yes!	10 Tell me some	15 Ch ch
2 Again	8 Is that right?	more then	With INFANT
3 Come on then	9 Well tell me	11 INFANT	16 Ahgoo
4 That's clever	some more then	12 Ooorrh	17 Goo
5 INFANT		13 Come on	
6 INFANT		14 Ch ch ch ch	
		With INFANT	

a century of research on the subject. We can use this knowledge to negotiate the roller coaster of baby's early emotional life through her preferred medium: music.

SINGING THROUGH A CRISIS

In the course of the past thirty years, I have met many momentarily miserable babies. For no apparent reason, the baby begins a steady crescendo (the musical term for growing louder and louder) of writhing and wailing. Neither the offer of a bottle nor a pacifier has any effect; the baby's cries are accelerating at an alarming rate and there is no end in sight. In these cases, the babies' distress quickly makes the parents equally upset. They fear that baby is either dismally failing her Baby Musicking class, or that it's somehow an indication of their own poor parenting. In these moments, most parents are so distressed that the situation can only worsen.

The solution consists of applying the fruit of the research that our baby whisperers began more than sixty years ago. This is not the moment for playful engagement in a question-and-answer game. The parents are going to need to establish a primal connection and bring baby back into the duet. This is a variation of the first duet that we can call the "first intervention."

The First Intervention

Position the anxious baby so that she is lying horizontally in the crook of your arm and can look directly into your face. Holding her firmly, almost squeezing, and rocking gently, try to match the cadence of her cries with the pace of your rocking and humming. You need to study and follow her breathing and movements, all the while keeping steady eye contact.

If you do this correctly, you will actually find yourself crying with your baby. When this happens, she begins to understand that you hear her, that you are matching her intentions, resonating with each other. This is the proof she needs to feel that she is not alone.

This moment of physical and vocal connection marks the beginning of the end of the crisis. Now you can begin to slow down your rhythm of rocking and humming to see if baby will follow. Begin to sing with descending musical intervals such as Sol-Mi, Fa-Re. These are the notes that mark the opening of Beethoven's dramatic Fifth Symphony. Think of the tatata *ta*, tatata *ta*, but imagine singing it very softly and slowly.

This downward melodic curve has a calming effect — as if baby has already understood that the conclusion of a conversation and a piece of music both involve a downward melodic movement — and when you can see this change come over her, you will experience both relief and perhaps surprise that you could accomplish this, simply by softly singing.

I've seen this process work almost instantly, or it can take a full five minutes, which is an entire day from an infant's perspective. Once the connection is established and we are out of crisis mode, I often use the musical name technique that we saw earlier with Max. Having a musical name for a child is a delightful way to connect and engage with baby. This musical engagement become synonymous with safety and pleasure in your child's mind. You can bring it out whenever you need to reconnect and reassure them in the wake of a trying situation.

These techniques for connecting with or calming your baby can be adapted and combined at almost any time, in any situation, to constantly maintain and strengthen the bond. Sometimes they are the only option: If you are in a car with baby strapped in the back seat or standing in front of a pot of boiling water, you cannot even turn around, let alone take her in your arms, without putting both of you at risk. If baby is getting fussy or, worse, seems ready to explode, bring out her musical name. Bring it out loud and clear and with gusto and repetition. Layer it atop baby's squawking, keep in sync with her cries, take a breath when she does — and you will see that this is often all she needs to settle down. Once you are vocally in sync, you will notice her relaxing, and the crisis will be over. If baby is perfectly happy, this duet will ensure that you get to your destination or cook that meal without her feeling alone and vulnerable.

Her calming down is an act of communication in and of itself. As she grows older, she will sing with you, or bang her spoon with you. For now, before her first birthday, she is mentally and emotionally participating in your duet, even if you cannot see or hear it. Recall that, as the "still face" experiment showed, babies will actually fight to get you back into the conversation if your attention strays. That is how strong the desire for communication is, beginning at birth.

Take comfort, too, in the fact that research indicates it is the *quality*, not the *quantity*, of these interactions that matters. When you find yourself worn out at the end of a long day, and your time with your baby is limited, this knowledge should empower you. It doesn't matter whether you think your nonsense lyrics are silly, or if you hate the sound of your own voice, or fear that you sing off-key; you will always be your baby's favorite vocal partner.

You are also a *necessary* partner. Remember that a baby needs to maintain a vocal lifeline to ensure his own safety. The more you engage in this vital proto-conversation, the more secure your baby will feel. A newborn baby's mind and body are fully ready for emotionally infused musical communication because both her hearing and her emotional centers are fully developed. When the music comes from you, firecrackers of happiness are firing in her burgeoning baby brain.

This may not feel like what you think of as a musical duet yet, because at the earliest stages, baby can't sing or dance with you. But rest assured that not only is she listening; she is also carefully observing and learning your every move. Very soon indeed she is even going to begin to show you what she wants by pointing to it. Then she will show you what she does *not* want by throwing it on the floor.

These too are major steps in a child's early development. We saw exactly this transformation in six-month-old Jacques, who was able to tell us what he wanted long before he had the ability to speak or even point.

LEARNING FROM THE BOTTOM UP

It was a dark and rainy winter morning in Paris. At L'École Koenig, parents, caretakers, and babies were taking off their coats and boots, getting ready for our Baby Musicking class. The pianist was already playing, and everyone was commiserating about the nasty weather. The teacher, Marion, was already seated on the edge of the bright red circle, waiting for everyone to join her, when Jacques, a six-month-old boy, was placed on the "magic circle" carpet. His nanny needed to leave Jacques on his own for a moment while she attended to Arthur, her other young charge. The class always begins with a repetitive rhythmic fragment, "doop doop WHAAA!" (short-short-long!). The fragment is sung, clapped, and stomped by everyone in a call-and-response format. At this point, Jacques had been attending his weekly music class for only two months, but that morning, as soon as he was seated, Jacques already knew what came next. He began to rock rhythmically back and forth, babbling something that sounded like "ah ah aaah."

Seeing this, and intuiting what Jacques was doing, Marion sat in front of him and began the song "doop doop whaaa," stomping her feet and clapping her hands. The pianist joined in, and Jacques's face lit up. He laughed, gurgled, and rocked back and forth, his eyes fixed on his teacher. He was trying to clap his hands as well, but they weren't quite matching up. We were all holding our breath. Jacques was glowing; he had made himself understood, he had gotten what he wanted: "doop doop whaaa!" He was so happy that he lost his balance and rolled over on the carpet. Marion laughed and picked Jacques up, and they danced together, singing "doop doop whaaa" as they spun around the room.

Scientists sometimes call what we had just seen *embodied cognition,* or learning through the body. Another term for learning through the body is *bottom-up.* Much of learning in early childhood happens this way, through the sensory experience of our bodies. Jacques had remembered the physical sensation of pleasure that had wrapped him like a warm blanket, and was asking to relive it. Jacques wanted to experience "doop doop whaaa" again because it made him happy! Jacques had no conscious awareness of any of this, but he pressed his face close to Marion's to connect with her and share his joy. Recognition of this mind-body-emotional connection is one of the most welcome and reassuring parts of scientific research in this field today.

The following week confirmed our previous observation. As soon as Jacques entered the room, still in his nanny's arms, he began bouncing up and down and intoning "ah ah aaah." He didn't wait this time. As soon as he sat down on the "magic circle" carpet, he held out his arms to Marion, begging to dance.

The number of connections taking place in Jacques's brain during this exchange is vertiginous; to think that fifty years ago, we thought that infants did not become fully human until they could speak. Jacques, after only seven sessions, had obviously remembered this small musical fragment. The short-short-long rhythm was embedded in Jacques's mind and body before he even had the motor skills necessary to reproduce it. In this case, music was reaching in and tickling Jacques's motor cortex. Moving in rhythm was quite challenging for him because he could barely sit up by himself, but the music was stimulating every inch of him, pushing him to muster just enough coordination to express what he was hearing and feeling.

Jacques was trying to show us what he wanted to do, and the success of his attempt was emotionally satisfying to him. So satisfying, in fact, that the first thing he "asked for" the following week was an encore! His charming example of Stephen Malloch's *communicative musicality* is replicated every day in our classrooms. Simply put, music and movement are a means of communication with very young children — long before the onset of language or the mastery of a musical instrument.

We now know that all of this babbling and movement we see in our children is part of the extraordinary singular period of development that occurs during the first year of life. The human brain is not an isolated computer sitting disconnected atop our bodies. The brain is the core of our central nervous system, part and parcel of our whole being. Body and mind are intimate co-workers, especially during the period of rapid growth and development in early life. This relationship can be observed among healthy babies, and also tragically with vulnerable children such as those in the Romanian orphanage. In places like that, there was no speaking, singing, or dancing, and infants were not encouraged or even allowed to move. There was no rhythmic, physical, or vocal connection with other human beings, and every aspect of the children's development was delayed or permanently stunted.

The more you engage vocally with your child, the happier you both will be. This is one of the delightful developmental effects of musical practice in early childhood. You never have to force children to babble or bang that spoon; in fact, you may sometimes have a hard time stopping them! These essential steps along the developmental path are so much fun, not to mention profoundly meaningful, precisely because they are shared between you and your baby.

OFF TO THE RACES

As your child moves into the second year of her life, she will accomplish two major milestones: she will walk and she will talk. The next chapter will explore the many ways music reinforces this magical audio-motor-linguistic dance taking place in your baby's brain during this exciting developmental stage. As we will see, the first duet begins to take on shape and form with the onset of language and physical coordination.

Even if you are aware that this will happen, I guarantee that your baby's musical babbling and boogying in the second year of life will take your breath away.

2 YEAR TWO
Babe on the Run

SCAN ME

URING A CONCERT IN OUR SCHOOL ONE spring Sunday, the fourteen-month-old sister of one of our music students escaped her parents' attention and began shuffling up the aisle, adorable in her bulging blue jumpsuit. Isabelle had been walking for only a short time, so she still had that uncertain wobble that goes with a baby's first steps. Everyone saw her, but no one had the heart to stop her. We all just watched and smiled as this little girl, fearless and independent, made her way up to the front of the room.

The next student to perform had just sat down at the piano as Isabelle drew closer to center stage. The young pianist launched into an upbeat bluesy piece with a swing rhythm. Isabelle stopped in her tracks, then began bending her knees and moving her diapered bottom wonderfully in time with the music. Her gesture was very jazzy, very natural, and very gutsy. We were all listening to the music but watching Isabelle. How could Isabelle, who had just learned to walk, have also learned to dance to a syncopated jazz rhythm?

The second year of life is marked by two extraordinary developments: walking and talking. Think of the number of things that need to be in place before baby can stand up and walk — lower back, leg and core muscle strength, left-right coordination, and of course the ability to balance. Balance, or equilibrium, depends on the inner ear. Would it surprise you to learn that music actually reaches in and tickles the inner ear, making our babies want to get up and groove?

Like walking, speaking involves a complex array of cognitive and muscular machinery whirring beneath the surface. A baby's first recognizable word always seems like a miracle. The closer we look at the cognitive and physical challenge of speaking, the more incredible this ability appears. But language, too, is connected with — and galvanized by — music.

This second chapter will help you understand the mechanisms behind the onset of language: when it begins, and how music and speech evolve together. Music, language, and movement are intimate partners during this vital developmental period. By understanding this complex audio-motor-linguistic waltz, you can happily sing and dance through the second year of life with your baby, laying the foundations for a sound body and a happy and healthy mind.

THE FIRST STEP

Baby's first steps along with baby's first words are two of the essential milestones in early life. Everyone remembers that extraordinary moment when baby puts her weight on one foot then on the other, and there it is: baby is walking. In this second year of life, baby is on the move, and she wants to move and groove with you. Music and movement are terrific friends, and the more play dates they have, the stronger their friendship grows.

Although I will give you many musical suggestions in this chapter, please keep in mind that you need no musical training to engage in a musical activity with your baby. You can always pick your favorite song and press the play button. Keep in mind, however, that this is not about passive listening — baby needs you to sing and dance with her. She will imitate you and probably invent moves of her own. This is one of the most enjoyable and potent activities that you can share with your child in her second year.

"Dancing" in infancy involves not only our innate musicality but also the child's need for movement, for the development of both body and mind. When babies move to music, clapping hands or stomping feet, they do this for their own pleasure, but they are also learning where their bodies begin and end, and how each part moves. The scientific term for this is *proprioception*. Coined by the English neurophysiologist C. S. Sherrington (1857–1952), "proprioception" combines the Latin *proprius* (my own) and the English "reception." It simply means knowing where one's own body parts are and what they are doing.

Proprioception is essential for a child's development. Without knowing where her hand is in relation to her mouth, a baby cannot feed herself. Without knowing where her foot is in relation to her other foot, an infant cannot learn to walk. Most of us are blissfully unaware of the requisite brain processes when we feel the urge to get up and move — but they form the foundation of all our actions.

When a toddler dances, her sense of where her body is in space and what that newly mobile body can do (proprioception) is reinforced with every move. This process is exponential; the confidence gleaned from lifting that little foot allows baby to take even more risks. It's a virtuous circle! No one needs to *learn* to dance; our bodies naturally want to move to music. It is no wonder that dancing is part of musical practice all over the world.

The desire to dance demonstrates health and happiness, and in turn, dancing with others contributes to baby's nascent prosocial behavior. Dancing requires awareness not only of one's body but also of the bodies and movements of others. We have all experienced the particular sensation of intimacy when dancing with a loved one or, sometimes, even with a total stranger. Dancing tunes us in to others in a specific visceral way. As we will soon see, this fine-tuning to others through dance, and the subsequent feeling of belonging, begins even before the onset of language. Sharing, caring, cooperating, and comforting are all elements of prosocial behavior. As with many aspects of infant development, science today situates the onset of this behavior very early in life.

Isabelle moved as though she had seen someone dance to a swing rhythm before. Her movements looked like the music sounded. This reminded me of a beautiful film made by Malloch and Trevarthen, the pathbreaking scientists whose work on infant musicality and communication I described in the previous chapter. The film shows a visually impaired Swedish baby choreographing the melody of the song her mother is singing, with a hand she cannot see. In Trevarthen's film, the baby looks like a tiny orchestral conductor, and yet she had never seen a conductor.

Likewise, our little Isabelle had never seen someone dance like this, nor had she heard this kind of music before. Nonetheless, she looked like a seasoned jazz singer on a bandstand. Where could this innate ability to move to music be coming from? How does it work? Recent fMRI imaging research suggests that the link between sound perception and our desire to move (auditory-motor coordination) involves multiple connections between the auditory and motor cortices, along with other specific areas of the brain. The cerebellum (Latin for "little brain") is very easy to spot; it looks like a small potato stuck to the bottom of the brain. This powerful little brain receives sensory information from its neighbor the spinal cord and coordinates voluntary movements. Another partner in the dance are the mysterious basal ganglia. The BG are actually a family of nuclei (plural of "nucleus") located deep inside the midbrain. One of the family members is the nucleus accumbens. Here the plot thickens: movement requires a physical effort. What could make our species systematically overcome laziness and want to get up and dance? It turns out that the basal ganglia are involved in motivation, reward, and even addiction! We want to move in part because there is a reward involved; movement makes us feel good! Impairment of the BG is one of the causes of Parkinson's disease, and not surprisingly, dance is one of the most enjoyable and successful therapies for Parkinson's patients.

Another area involved in our desire to dance is the vestibular system, one of the oldest parts of the brain in evolutionary terms and one of the first to develop. Research has found links between the vestibular system and such seemingly disparate developmental abilities as proprioception, balance, physical confidence, and reading. I have chosen to focus on this part of the audio-motor waltz because our increasingly sedentary lifestyle is affecting the healthy development of this vital system in young children. This is not a vague hypothesis; we already see the effects in our classrooms.

THE VESTIBULAR SYSTEM

The vestibular system is a group of interconnected compartments located in the inner ear. This sophisticated system sits atop the cochlea, our tiny snail-shaped hearing organ that is part of our auditory system. Within the vestibular system are three semicircular canals filled with a fluid called endolymph. When we move our head, the fluid moves through the canals according to our movements. The canals detect specific movements — up and down, side to side, and back and forth. The vestibular system uses two other organs, called the otolith organs, to detect acceleration, gravitational forces, and tilting movements. The vestibular system allows us to keep our balance; stabilize our head, body, and eyes during movement; and maintain posture. It is a tiny, invisible state-of-the-art control tower, guiding our bodies from dawn to dusk!

Without a functioning vestibular system, we can't sit up, let alone walk or dance.

The vestibular system ensures that our eyes can stay focused during the multitude of movements we make every day. Without it, we cannot even nod our head, not to mention stand up without losing our balance, because the world would appear to be spinning. The vestibular system accomplishes this by sending electrical signals to the neural structures that control eye movements and to the muscles that keep us upright.

Without the vestibular system regulating our eye movements, we also cannot learn to read. This is because our vestibular system allows our eyes to stay focused while our bodies are moving — and our bodies are constantly moving, even when we think we are standing still. A child with an underdeveloped vestibular system will experience the letters on the page as if they were floating around, virtually swimming. Sadly, today we are seeing more and more of these types of reading difficulties among urban children who are required to sit at a desk for an inappropriate amount of time — or worse, who have been parked too often in front of screens.

Like all of our faculties, the vestibular system develops through use — or practice. We begin practicing all of our extraordinary physical capacities even before birth. This is what leads to our ability to fend for ourselves and thus survive. This is why children move; they need and love action and can never get enough of it. The more our babies move, the more they develop their vital vestibular system, as well as the muscles that lead to the control of posture and mobility.

The link between music and the vestibular system is, of course, the ear. We hear music through our ears, but we feel it in our bodies. Music enters the brain through our auditory system, and the brain relays the information via electrical signals, triggering activity in all the components that make up our incredible audio-motor waltz. Our vestibular system has one of the leading roles in this fascinating process. The music that Isabelle was hearing created a need to move. She was spontaneously choreographing the music she was hearing and feeling, blissfully unaware of all the extraordinary processes taking place in her baby brain and body.

When we see children move and dance in early childhood, we are amazed and delighted, and often label these children "musical." Sadly, children who do not clap in rhythm, sing in tune, or make beautiful dance moves are labeled "non-musical," but nothing could be further from the truth. Congenital amusia, or "tone deafness," is an extremely rare phenomenon afflicting between 1.5 to 4.0 percent of our population according to a recent study.

Children are naturally attracted to music, and as with speech, the more they are exposed to it, the more they integrate its fundamental structures. The isochronous pulsation (steady beat) is a musical universal and one of the first things infants respond to. We see children striving to move with others in musical activity very early in life — even if their efforts are not entirely successful. When children seem oblivious to the rhythms and gestures surrounding them, this reflects not a lack of musical talent or congenital amusia but, more likely, a physiological or psychological challenge. For instance, it could indicate that the child's vestibular system needs a boost. When the vestibular system is not adequately developed, indeed children will have difficulty with all forms of coordination and concentration. Insufficient vestibular development can also impede a child's development of physical confidence, making them fearful or even accident prone. Happily, the vestibular system can be boosted with targeted physical therapy, which is noninvasive and which can even be enjoyable for the child, especially when music is involved.

Elena was a curly-haired, rosy-cheeked, gentle eighteen-month-old when she entered our school. She was an only child, and her parents wanted her to have music in her life at a very early age. She was a cherubic and affectionate little girl, and one could not help but hug her when she reached out her arms, which she did often.

Within a few weeks, we began to notice that Elena was having difficulty sitting up on her own, something babies generally master within the first year. She would either be leaning against another child or against the wall. If neither was available, she would lie down on the floor. This annoyed the other children, which in turn upset Elena, who would inevitably melt into a sobbing little lump of misery.

We were seeing a potentially destructive pattern in the making, so with her parents' permission, I took Elena's case to a medical doctor and an occupational therapist to find an explanation for her behavior. The answers I got would highlight how integral vestibular development is to a child's development overall.

Elena had difficulty sitting up on her own, one of the first indicators of insufficient vestibular development. This also made it difficult for her to understand where her body was in space; hence her inability to dance with the other children. I was relieved to learn that Elena did not need drugs or psychological therapy, both of which would be inappropriate at her age. She simply needed to jump, hop on one foot, throw and catch a ball, swirl to the right and swirl to the left, and so on. In short, she needed to move.

A child like Elena doesn't lean against a wall or another child because she wants to but because she needs the physical support. Her vestibular system, proprioception, and postural muscles are not yet sufficiently developed. There are so many problems linked to insufficient development of this system that children can be misdiagnosed as having chronic attention deficiency or reading disabilities, when in fact it is their bodies and inner ears that need attention. Dr. Carla Hannaford, author of *Smart Moves: Why Learning Is Not All in Your Head*, notes: "In Denmark, fifty percent of children between ages two and a half and six are in Forest Kindergartens where they climb rocks, trees, hills, roll, jump, balance and play at least four hours a day no matter the weather. These children's vestibular systems are so well developed that learning difficulties and dyslexia are rare." Not all children, of course, are so lucky — but music can make up the difference.

MOVEMENT SONGS

Most parents and teachers have a basic awareness of early vestibular developmental benchmarks. Children are generally able to sit up on their own beginning at around six months. They pull themselves upright (with support) around nine months and begin walking independently between eight and eighteen months.

Later benchmarks, however, tend to be less well known. For example, a child of four should be able to stand on one foot for a few seconds; this can happen once the vestibular system is ready to provide visual focus and equilibrium. At four, children should be able to recognize and possibly even write their own name; this requires that their eyes remain focused in spite of their bodies' constant movements, a feat that is supported by the vestibular system. Likewise, when a child cannot cross over the front of her body with her hand, from left to right or vice versa, this indicates that she may not be ready to write. Writing requires passing from left to right across the center of the body (crossing the midline).

The majority of children develop physically on schedule, but our lifestyles and even safety measures have evolved over the past decades in ways that sometimes interfere with little ones' development. Some children today, especially those who grow up in big cities, need an extra boost to allow them to feel confident in their bodies. Simple and enjoyable games such as passing a beanbag, playing hopscotch, or singing "movement songs" can be entertaining ways to help your child develop these important abilities. Collectively these interventions are known as *vestibular rehabilitation*.

The first proponents of vestibular rehabilitation were two British doctors, Harold Cooksey and Sir Terence Cawthorne, who published a series of exercises in 1946 to help soldiers recuperate balance after sustaining war injuries. For many years this was the only material available. There has been a steady increase in research since the 1960s. Today there are entire organizations and educational programs dedicated to research and training in vestibular rehabilitation.

The official term for this therapy is *vestibular rehabilitation therapy,* or VRT. For adults, VRT is an exercise-based program designed to reduce vertigo and dizziness, gaze instability, and even motion sickness. The rehab is also movement-based for children, but the goal is to wake up a sleepy system. This workout increases the child's physical abilities and confidence, allowing her to move and take calculated risks. Before therapy, the prospect of jumping off even a low surface is daunting. When treatment is successful, we see the difference very quickly. There is still a slight hesitation — the internal dialogue is visible in the child's facial expression: "Can I jump off this rock? It looks like fun . . . Here I go!"

Vestibular rehabilitation therapy for children is a new and fast-growing field. Yet practitioners have encountered a number of difficulties along the way. One of the problems is that while adults can readily communicate about the problem they are experiencing, and submit to voluntary therapy, children are often unaware that things are not as they should be. The child has no reference point. She cannot possibly know that the dizziness she experiences when she moves her head up and down is not normal; she has never known any other sensation. And identifying the problem is only the first challenge. The next, more considerable challenge is to engage children in such a way that they will complete a session of VRT therapy. Too often the prescribed activities simply feel like work — and children treat them accordingly.

It seems obvious to me that we need to find a way for children to love their therapy sessions, and I believe we can do this with music and movement — the earlier the better. If we could associate the physical exercises that children need for vestibular development with the natural and joyful stimulation that music creates in their audio-motor system, it would be the ultimate win-win.

But it also seems obvious to me that this win-win needn't be confined to vestibular rehabilitation therapy. Since we now know how this vital system works, why would we wait to see if a child needs therapy? Why not just consider this a part of our children's overall development, like learning to swim or ride a bicycle?

As I learned more about the vestibular system, I decided to create a body of musical material that would encourage specific movements that are important for vestibular development, which we could introduce to children as early as possible, specifically in the second year of life, when walking begins. Using the songs that I composed, we could engage children in a fun-filled musical moment while helping their vestibular systems flourish.

You do not have to be a highly trained musician or a physical therapist to engage in movement songs with your baby. The key is not your expertise but your loving participation and your sense of fun. Once you understand the science behind each movement song, you will probably feel very motivated. The following two exercises will show you how fun and easy these songs can be for you and your baby.

I Am a Windmill

The "Windmill" song is for balance, crossing the midline (the middle of the body), and eye movement stabilization. As with all the original music mentioned in this book, the score for this song can be found in the appendix. The recordings can be found at JoanKoenig.com.

Stand behind your baby and gently guide her right hand down to her left foot, while singing:

I am a windmill, I touch my toes.

Help her move back up and touch her nose with the index fingers of both hands, and sing:

I am a windmill, I touch my nose.

Do this twice, the second time with her left hand to her right foot.

Now pick up your child, place her on your hip, and encourage her to hold out her arms while singing "Turn and turn and turn and turn . . . ," and spin in one direction, then the other. To add to the fun, try making a game of maintaining eye contact while you are spinning, or give your child scarves to hold in her hands while she swirls. If your child is walking, you can hold her hands and help her do this on her own.

Finally, repeat the beginning of the song:

I am a windmill, I touch my toes.
I am a windmill, I touch my nose.

It is fascinating to observe the natural stages of vestibular development. Children who have only just started walking do not cross their bodies; they bend down, right hand to right foot. They will learn to cross over with practice. It is exciting to think that something so enjoyable and fun for them is also ensuring healthy vestibular development.

These movement songs are an extension of the first duet we studied in chapter 1. Even though she may be walking on her own, your baby still needs to move together with you. As with the win-win of Motherese, the pleasure we feel when we dance together makes us want to dance more, and the more we move, the more we develop this vital part of our inner ear, our equilibrium. Not only are you both having fun, but also you are using what science teaches us about vestibular development to ensure that your baby is exercising this important system early in life. Practicing these targeted movement songs in the earliest years of children's lives could have enduring benefits — for your child's vestibular system as well as her physical confidence.

Understanding the vestibular system and its importance in early childhood development makes the relatively recent dichotomy between music and dance seem all the more absurd. Many languages don't have separate words for music and dance, and music is rarely made without dance. In most parts of the world, people go to community events to create and share music with one another, and movement is part of the experience. Families of balafon and djembe masters accompany village dancing in Mali, and in the Basque region of France and Spain, spontaneous a cappella choirs unite young and old in village festivities. In short, people love to come out to play, sing, and dance together — but they get a chance to do so only when it is part of their culture, and too often, in the twenty-first century, it is not.

The delightful social function of music does not occur, for instance, when we are required to sit quietly in concert halls. The tradition of "classical" music in the West, indeed, has taken a separate path from other musical forms that still include participation and movement. This path has led to an increasing professionalization of musical practice and, sadly, to less and less music making in homes and communities. The result today is that when parents think about music for their children, they think of music classes instead of imagining just singing, moving, and shaking with their babies.

Speaking of shaking, the next exercise is for vestibular development, and it is guaranteed to have you, your child, and probably your entire family in stitches.

Shake and Stop Theme and Variations

Stand with your (walking) child holding one hand and begin the song slowly and with suspense:

I'm going to . . . shake, shake, shake: one foot in the air

  shake, shake, shake: une main par terre
  [one hand on the floor]

  shake, shake, shake: two feet in the air

At the first "shake," really let go and shake; then when the recording stops, or when you stop singing, stay as still as a statue, holding one foot in the air until you decide to give the cue to start on the second phrase. A child under two cannot stand on one foot alone, so you will need to hold her hand. She will proudly lift one little foot in the air and try to hold it there.

The second verse, *"une main par terre,"* requires children to touch the floor with one hand in the air and one hand on the floor. Ideally, your child looks like a little triangle. The third verse, "two feet in the air," requires jumping! The likelihood of falling down (which occurs often in the classroom, and I suspect voluntarily) only enhances the experience for you and your child. If your baby is not yet walking, hold her in your arms and do the movements yourself. With baby in your arms this is quite the workout! She will experience it all with you — the leg lifting, the hand on the floor, and the jumping, even in this position.

Children love these activities and will probably ask to repeat them daily. This is as joyful as it is beneficial: the more she balances on one foot, jumps in the air, or hangs upside down from a branch, the more she strengthens her vital vestibular system. No therapy sessions required.

THE FIRST WORD

The extraordinary physical developments taking place in the second year of life are not the only quasi-miracle you will witness during this exciting year. Baby will also begin to speak.

Most babies pronounce their first words during their second year of life, and these are memorable moments, to say the least. I can still remember standing in a bucolic, bovine-filled pasture in Burgundy, when suddenly out of my son's mouth came a perfectly pronounced "cow." The extent of his vocabulary up to that point had been "mapa." It felt like a miracle! But in truth, it was anything but.

What is happening in her brain before baby utters her first recognizable word? The research in this field offers some compelling findings. Language skills are developing long before that magical first word, and music fine-tunes baby's aural skills if practiced during this preverbal period.

The musicality of language that we observe in Motherese in the earliest days of infancy continues well into the second year of life. Parents speak to their infants with musical intonations, and you will rarely hear an eighteen-month-old child speak in a monotone voice (unless they are pretending to be a robot). Children make the most amazing musical sounds when learning to talk. When children are vocalizing or babbling, it usually sounds much more like music than speech. When analyzed acoustically, we see rhythmic patterns and actual musical forms such as introduction, development, climax, and coda.

Parents everywhere often imitate these enchanting sounds, eager to engage in this preverbal conversation. Baby is now officially speaking in what scientists call "prelinguistic non-cry vocalizations" — or, more simply, babbling. But when the baby begins a specific phase of babbling called "canonic babbling," in which she puts together two linguistic building blocks called phonemes and begins to play with them, the label "prelinguistic" begins to slip off.

This is a huge milestone in the child's development of language. A phoneme is the *sound* of a vowel or a consonant. Phonemes are language specific. French baby babbling contains longer vowel sounds, while American baby babbling contains shorter, flatter vowel sounds. Babies will produce seemingly endless repetitions of the sound of the letter "m" — *mmmmmmmmmm...* — before adding a vowel and producing "mamamamamama" for what can feel like hours. Soon enough the mellifluous combinations of consonants and vowels slowly metamorphose into recognizable words.

A rhythmic element underscores this canonic babbling. When baby begins "Ga ga Gaa" or "Ba ba Baa," listen carefully and you will begin to hear that the sounds are often repeated with exactly the same rhythm. "Ga ga Gaa" is short-short-long (or two eighth notes and a quarter note). The babies are not consciously trying to repeat these rhythms; they do so instinctively because repetition is necessary for memory retention.

A baby's need for repetition is physical as well as cognitive — she is practicing. Babies will repeat their first phonemes and syllables for what seems like hours on end. In doing so they are actually training the many muscles that are necessary for articulation.

Repetition and predictability are found in rhythm and language alike. Children need to be able to discern rhythm and predict patterns in language. This is part of what will enable them to distinguish separate words in a sentence and begin to integrate syntax. Children practice their preverbal skills in precisely the same way that musicians practice their scales, over and over again, preparing themselves for the physical and cognitive demands of the language they will speak or the music they will play.

In this second phase of language acquisition, parents and siblings often begin to realize that the sounds the child endlessly repeats actually mean something to her. This is already a benchmark. In most cases it means that the child is labeling an object. Even if the label is not a real word, baby has understood the concept of naming something. It works, because after countless repetitions and insistence, we slow-witted adults finally understand what the invented word means.

When my daughter was eighteen months old, we began to notice how often she said "wadidi." We loved the word and smothered her with kisses every time she said it. It took some time for us to realize that "Wadidi" was what she called her brother, Aurélien. Frankly, who can blame her; the name is tough to pronounce, but she had gotten the number of syllables right. We also began to understand that "bezine" meant "finished" or *"fini,"* and "badzabats" meant "lollipop." The accents and the number of syllables were spot-on, even if the rest was a mystery.

The musical counterpart to syllables and accentuation is rhythm. In the case of Wadidi/Aurélien, this is a triplet. Bezine/*fini,* or finished, would be two quarter notes, with an accent on the second note; coincidentally, this also sounds a bit like "the end." She got quite fancy with "badzabats": the first syllable was a long "baa," the middle syllable a very short "za," and the last was a percussive "bats."

Babbling in early childhood sounds more like music than actual

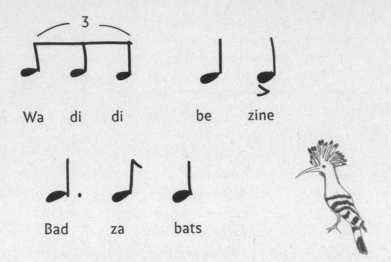

speech. The baby brain has not yet separated music from speech. We tend to think of practicing and improvisation happening only in music, but this is a clear example of the overlap of music and language. This is musically enhanced speech practicing, which children do naturally and spontaneously. They are improvising and practicing simultaneously, playing with the ingredients that will soon transform into speech.

THE PHONEME OF THE OPERA

Most of us have already experienced an overlap between music and speech. The words to a song we learned in early childhood will come back to us effortlessly, and with absolute clarity, decades later. Sometimes these lyrics are even in a foreign language that we do not speak!

There is a certain popular fascination with this overlap; for instance, you might remember the film *The King's Speech*, where the future King George VI of England overcomes his debilitating stutter by singing. But there is a plethora of serious scientific research about this phenomenon as well.

In 2008 the eminent specialist Aniruddh Patel, professor of psychology at Tufts University, published an award-winning book, *Music, Language, and the Brain*. His research includes the links between rhythm perception and speech, as well as emotional communication in both music and speech. He has also investigated how other animals process music as a research window into the evolutionary foundations of music cognition.

In 2012 Professor Patel synthesized his findings about the parallel brain circuitry of music and speech into what he calls — appropriately enough — the OPERA hypothesis.

O is for *overlap*. There is an anatomical overlap in the brain networks that process shared acoustic features present in music and speech.
P is for *precision*. Music actually requires more precision in processing than speech.
E is for *emotion*. Musical activities produce pleasure and strong positive emotions.
R is for *repetition*. The musical activities that solicit this network are frequently repetitive in nature, as is early babbling.
A is for *attention*. Musical activities that activate this network require and facilitate focused attention.

A hypothesis is not a theory — it is an idea that has not yet been formally proven. However, after thirty-five years of musicking with young children, I wholeheartedly confirm Patel's hypothesis. The immediate *attention* that even babies display as soon as we play an instrument or sing to them in person is extraordinary. They stop moving and only seem to breathe again once the music has stopped; then they wave their arms and legs, visibly asking for an encore. When they are old enough to begin babbling and tapping on a drum, they will *repeat* their experimentation ad nauseam. They are practicing and loving every minute — even if *you* are ready to throw the drum out the window. Music provokes a strong, visible, and immediate *emotional* response in children. They will stop in their tracks when they hear live music, and when they participate in a musical activity, this will be the first thing they tell their parents about after class. We can see the impact of music in their expressions long before they have the words to express their emotions. Once they can talk about the feelings music provokes, their stories are often very moving. One of my favorite quotes is from a little five-year-old boy: "This song makes me feel sad, but I'm smiling!" We had the pleasure of explaining the concept of nostalgia after this memorable moment. The *precision* necessary for music making is without equal; being "off" by even a nanosecond will spoil the piece, and even the youngest child will notice. I can only presume that the brain is getting quite the precision workout to keep up. The *overlap* between music and language is perhaps the most mysterious and poignant aspect of Patel's hypothesis. When children are first learning to speak, their babbling sounds more like music than speech. Popular songs have people all over the world singing in a foreign tongue, and older people who have lost the ability to speak can still sing the songs of their youth.

Patel's research suggests that the aural fine-tuning developed in musical practice is so precise that it actually benefits speech and literacy. His research on rhythm patterns in speech and music indicates that rhythmic sensitivity is necessary for linguistic development. When a child has difficulty with rhythmic sensitivity, speech and reading problems such as dyslexia can occur. Conversely, many children sharpen their rhythmic sensitivity by blending phonemes in the style of babbling appropriately described as "canonic babbling." The canon in music is of course the song that goes on and on.

Most children naturally begin their phase of canonic babbling with what I call a "Phoneme Symphony." This babbling sounds like music, and it can go on for hours on end. Even at this early stage, babies are practicing making sounds that reflect their native language. You can encourage and engage baby with the following activity, a simple repetitive vocal and rhythmic game by the same name.

The Phoneme Symphony

This is a call-and-response game with simple phonemes. Sit down cross-legged in front of your baby and create a steady beat by rocking from left to right. You can also tap your hands on your knees.

Now start singing with a simple short-short-long rhythm. Keep your pulse steady and sing *a a aa* repeatedly, with any melody or intonation you like.

Then switch to *e e ee*. You will feel your facial muscles moving; when you pronounce the long *e* sound you have to smile!

When you sing *a a aa*, baby will do her best to repeat — even if her response is not yet entirely audible. When you switch to *e e ee*, you will see that she registers the change in your facial expression *and* the sound.

Now try *p pp p* with a long-short-short-long rhythm — exaggerating the popping *p* sound with your facial expression. Then you can begin mixing them up. Soon, she can be the leader and you will play the role of the phoneme detective. It doesn't matter if your baby does not join in at the beginning — she may just want to observe! She will join in with time. Watch and listen carefully; she may be telling you that she wants to play the game without you even prompting her.

With this simple verbal tennis game, you are gently strengthening both her rhythmic and phonetic awareness, which we now know are important factors in language and literacy. What's more, this game can evolve along with your child; as your baby grows out of the initial simple sounds, you can begin to experiment with all kinds of syllables and rhythms. You can even go wild with a *Ti Ti Tatata Boo!*

Why do some children have high-level language skills while others struggle? Patricia Kuhl, the co-director of the Institute for Learning and Brain Sciences at the University of Washington in Seattle, has proposed one answer, drawing on a pathbreaking study that reveals the vital role that human partnership plays in language acquisition — a finding that has powerful implications for music as well.

In 1992 Kuhl set up a study in which six-month-old children were tested for speech perception with a head-turning test, a standard baby-testing procedure. The babies are on their parents' laps, and the parents wear sound-reduction headphones so as not to influence the babies. A series of phonemes are played from a speaker in the room, something like a string of *p, p, p, p, p,* and then a *d.* When the baby turns her head at the sound of the new phoneme, this indicates that she has heard it. The same children were then tested at thirteen, sixteen, and twenty-four months of age to assess their language development.

The results demonstrated a direct correlation between the perception of phonemes at six months of age and language skills at the age of two. These skills included word comprehension, word production, and general understanding. The babies who noticed the subtle phonetic changes at the age of six months had developed better language skills by age two than the babies who did not hear the differences. Kuhl and her team concluded that the ability to perceive phonemes at the age of six months is a significant indicator of a child's future linguistic development.

In 1997, during the Clinton presidency, Kuhl was invited to the White House Conference on Early Childhood Development and Learning. When she presented her work, along with her conclusion that infants learn by listening long before they can speak, the president pricked up his ears. Clinton, aware of the increasingly poor language skills among children in the United States, asked Kuhl exactly how and when babies develop strong language skills. Kuhl said she wasn't sure, but perhaps if Clinton gave her the funding, she could find out.

Clinton gave her the grant, and she designed a surprising study in which nine-month-old babies in the United States received twelve short Mandarin Chinese "lessons." One group was read to and spoken with by Kuhl's Mandarin-speaking doctoral students. A second group was shown videos of Mandarin speakers reading and talking. The result was clear and compelling: the children who had a human teacher interacting with them demonstrated sensitivity to the Mandarin phonemes. The children who had video lessons learned nothing. Nine-month-old babies learned to recognize and distinguish the sounds of a new language, but only when the lessons came via another person.

Kuhl's study demonstrates that human contact, or what she calls "social gating," is the essential ingredient in language acquisition. This is consistent with Jerome Bruner and Colwyn Trevarthen's findings that we saw in the first chapter of this book. With the addition of Patel's OPERA hypothesis, a simple recipe for strong language skills emerges — constant playful vocal and musical interactions, beginning at birth.

Unfortunately, instead of following this simple recipe, we continue to disassociate language learning from music making when in fact they need to happen at the same time and in the same way — through oral transmission, movement, and playful interactions with loved ones.

This is real science, not a myth — an important distinction when it comes to describing music's developmental benefits. We need to be wary of what scientists have dubbed "soft science" or "neuromyths," of which there are many in circulation. The baby edutainment industry has been churning out products that purport to teach your infant foreign languages, math and music, and more, just by sitting in front of a screen. There is only one small problem: most learning in infancy requires human contact, and Professor Kuhl has proved it. Children learn less efficiently from passive exposure without human contact, or in some cases do not learn from it at all. And yet the neuromyth that babies benefit from passive exposure to language and music persists more than twenty years later.

MOZART SCHMOZART

Even today, parents tell me that they have heard about the cognitive boost that babies get from listening to Mozart. Unfortunately, they've been misled by one of the greatest musical fallacies in modern neuroscience. The "Mozart effect" is a perfect example of how quickly a neuromyth bonfire can be lit, and how difficult it is to extinguish.

In 1993 Frances Rauscher and colleagues from the Center for the Neurobiology of Learning and Memory, at the University of California, published a study in the British scientific journal *Nature*. The paper claimed that college students demonstrated enhanced performance on an exam after listening to Mozart. This finding sparked a whole industry of books, CDs, and related products that claimed to

— among other things — teach children foreign languages or simply make them magically smarter. There was just one problem: the underlying finding didn't stand up to scrutiny.

The misguided public hype surrounding the "Mozart effect" was greeted with both annoyance and a good measure of humor in the scientific community. In 1999 the American psychologist Christopher Chabris published "Prelude or Requiem for the 'Mozart Effect'?" in the very same journal, *Nature*. In a 2010 review of this phenomenon in the journal *Intelligence*, three scientists from the University of Vienna published their study, charmingly titled "Mozart Effect — Schmozart Effect: A Meta-Analysis." Both research teams demonstrated that it was impossible to replicate the results announced by Rauscher. In the meantime, though, the mythical "Mozart effect" had become big business, while also generating a lot of confusion.

The only really valuable takeaway from this phenomenon is the emotional factor. If we like what we are listening to, whether it be Mozart, Elvis, or heavy metal, we feel good and are likely to do just about anything with more ease than if we are unhappy. This could help to explain the improved performance seen in the original study. But it doesn't mean that there is any lasting effect on listeners — let alone on developing minds.

The "Mozart effect" initially claimed that it was the structure of a specific piano concerto that increased certain cognitive abilities in the listeners. Even if Mozart's music contained hidden superpowers, it is unlikely that a young child would be affected. Merely listening to recorded music does not involve active exchange with another person. Learning in early childhood is based on this duet — which, as Patricia Kuhl's Mandarin study demonstrated, is a precondition for learning.

A real "Mozart effect" would be inviting a group of children to sing and dance — for instance, to the beautiful Papageno aria from *The Magic Flute*. It's a Mozart composition — but it's "effective" only when you engage with it in a certain way.

"Pa pa papapapa pa pa ..." Papageno the bird catcher and his newfound love Papagena begin their courtship with a duet: the only

word is the syllable *pa* for the first sixteen measures. It contains an engaging rhythmic structure that accelerates from one syllable per four beats to the same syllable repeated so quickly that it is almost a tongue twister.

Infants love this absurd and lovely aria and will ask to "sing" it over and over again. They like it not because it's Mozart but because it has a simple melody, a single repeated phoneme, and an accelerating rhythmic pattern much like those we find in nursery rhymes, or in children's improvised "Phoneme Symphonies."

The Papageno aria is fun and it's funny, an ideal piece of music to play with — but do not confuse pushing the play button with an actual musical experience. It is vital to remember that as with every musical moment shared with your child, it is the physical engagement of musicking with you that matters. Children do not learn through passive exposure — you need to *be* Papageno!

Throw away the baby genius materials; your baby wants to learn from you. You don't need to be a musician or a linguist — above all, you need to be you. As we saw with Daniel and his frustration with "baby music," you will feel most comfortable and free if you are singing and dancing to music you love and doing so whenever the mood strikes, instead of waiting for some scheduled "music time."

The following exercises can help you include music and movement in day-to-day life. But most importantly, they are intended to help you create a musical moment with, and for, your child.

Flying Potatoes

Babies love to play the age-old game of opening their mouths while you make the food-laden spoon fly into it. You can spice up this ritual with a little help from Freddie Mercury and Queen's iconic "We Will Rock You."

You may recall that this short-short-long rhythm was originally intended to invite audience participation with "stomp-stomp-*clap*." In my experience, this is a rhythmic segment that children — and adults — immediately respond to.

Start with a "stomp-stomp-*clap*" yourself. Your baby is most likely going to begin to tap her spoon on the highchair or begin waving her arms along with you. Since you are going to be feeding baby, you can stomp with your two feet, and instead of clapping your hands together, you can tap on your thigh or the kitchen counter with your free hand.

Now make those potatoes fly high in the sky and into baby's mouth with only slightly modified lyrics: "We will, we will . . . eat you! Eat you!" As soon as the spoon is in baby's mouth, stop singing until she begins to chew, which she will do first out of sheer surprise, and then to make sure that you continue this hilarious routine. Keep going: "We will, we will, chew you" and "We will, we will swallow you."

Oh Soap!

Bath time is also a lovely moment for this kind of fun. You can pretend to lose the soap in the bath to the tune of the Beatles' "Hey Jude."

Oh soap
Where you have you gone?
I need baby to go and find you!
You're slippery and oh so hard to see
But clever baby will bring you to me.

You can make an infinite number of variations: the rubber duck or the shampoo can go missing, and even baby can hide under a towel. Don't get stuck on matching the music perfectly; be flexible and creative. You will quickly see that any silly song you come up with today will be the first thing your baby asks for tomorrow.

These musical moments are more precious than ever in our hectic twenty-first-century world. It's a common observation that our lives have changed more in the last one hundred years than in the two thousand years before that. We live with complications and distractions that our forebears could never have imagined. How can we provide a solid start for our children in such a frantic environment? It might seem impossible. But the answers are there if we look back far enough.

Our ancestors practiced music together in families and communities. Music was never practiced without movement, and even infants participated. Children did not go to music classes; they made music with their parents and their extended families.

You too can tap into this life-affirming natural phenomenon. All you have to do is set aside your inhibitions and tune in to the music you love, whatever it is. I have had children come to school telling me about all kinds of musical experiences, including going to concerts, hearing music in church, or seeing street musicians. The experiences they enjoy most involve singing and dancing with their parents.

Learning to walk and learning to talk both happen in this extraordinary second year of your child's life, and music is an integral part of both processes. Indeed, never are the links between music, movement, and language more apparent than at this age. Throughout our lives, rhythm and melody underscore both movement and language, but the two are practically indistinguishable during this developmental phase. Every move and sound that baby makes creates a spark that in turn ignites more musical and linguistic development.

You have an essential role to play in this process. Your baby is hardwired to learn, and she wants nothing more than to dance and sing with her favorite partner: you!

THE MUSIC AND MAGIC OF INVENTION

As she moves into her third year, your child will begin inventing stories, a process that will be enriched — or even triggered — by music. Your child's brain is still highly emotional and blissfully free of critical judgment. Now these emotions are seeking creative expression. Musical exploration is the perfect medium for this. When given the opportunity, all children invent musical soundtracks to their stories. In the coming year, music will also promote critical capacities like self-control and focus — all of which are vital to both social integration and lifelong happiness.

3 YEAR THREE
Body and Soul

SCAN ME

MAXIME, A SWEET TWO-AND-A-HALF-YEAR-old boy, began attending our Baby Musicking class one September. His mother, Victoire, was terribly excited about the class because of her passion for classical music. She was not a musician herself, but she had worked for a world-renowned classical pianist, and this daily exposure to music had been life-changing for her. Her enthusiasm was extraordinary, and she was more than willing to take a morning off from work to accompany Maxime to the class. I could tell right away that I'd be able to count on her to jump in and dance, helping dispel any shyness among the other adults. I did not expect that her son would need as much if not more encouragement than the other children —at least at first.

On the first day of class, Victoire settled into her place in the circle with her little son nestled on her lap — a perch from which Maxime proceeded to watch the entire session. He barely participated, and even declined my invitation to come to the piano and improvise. I could sense Victoire's disappointment. She had been so excited for the class; why wasn't her son enthusiastic about it too?

After the class, I reassured Victoire that Maxime was going through a natural phase. He needed to observe before participating. This seemed to mollify her. But then several weeks went by with much the same behavior. Maxime would smile, and seemed to be enjoying the class, but when asked to do something specific, such as playing the piano, the xylophone, or the harp, he'd decline.

I was more worried about Victoire at this point than about Maxime. I have seen many children watch and wait for a long time before participating — and when they do finally decide to join in, sometimes it feels as though they have been practicing the entire time. But like so many parents, Victoire lacked my experience and basis for comparison. She must be crushed, I thought. But I was wrong.

At the end of the class one day, when I went to reassure Victoire once again, she stopped me with a smile. "Can I show you something?" She proceeded to show me a three-minute video in which Maxime went through an accelerated version of the entire music class at home.

In the recording, Maxime began with the "Stand Up" motif — a single upward glissando on the piano. (A glissando, or "sliding" in Italian, means that the player literally slides their hand up the instrument with no attention to individual notes.) This simple motif is used to indicate that it's time to stand up. Maxime waved his tiny hand across his own keyboard from left to right (lower to higher notes), all the while ordering his parents to stand up: *"Debout!"* He then played an approximation of the "Sit Down" music, which is roughly the same motif as the iconic first notes of Beethoven's Fifth Symphony: "tatata *ta*," or "sit sit sit down." This is the motif we use when it's time to stop dancing and sit down. The children love it when we play the motifs faster and faster — "Stand Up/Sit Down" — until they fall into a giggling heap on the floor.

I was delighted to see that Maxime had spontaneously translated the words "stand up" into the French *"debout,"* because the terms have the same number of syllables in both languages — whereas he did not translate the "Sit Down" motif into French, because the French translation is complicated and would not have matched the rhythm. Maxime made this choice instinctively and effortlessly, in a vivid display of what Patricia Kuhl calls "the linguistic genius of babies."

He then proceeded to teach his parents to recognize and name the sound of "Do-domino" — part of a pitch recognition game that we often play at L'École Koenig. We begin these pitch recognition games very early, by presenting the notes as having names and distinct personalities, just like people. The music for the note Do is a catchy swing motif that Maxime sang perfectly in rhythm.

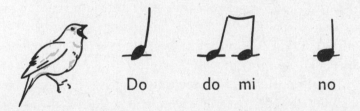

In the video Victoire was showing me, Maxime also played "Do-domino" on his piano, with both hands, the way he had seen our pianist play it. Of course it was not the actual music, but it was a perfectly recognizable approximation. The gestures, and therefore the rhythm, were spot-on. Maxime even showed his parents how they should tap their hands on the floor, the dance movement we make for "Do-domino." When his parents identified the pitch by singing "Do-domino," Maxime beamed, clapped his hands, and said, "Yes!"

Maxime was not only sharing something pleasurable with his parents; he also was teaching them something new, which meant that he felt a degree of mastery, even at the young age of two and a half. In a few short weeks, at this early age, he had absorbed the melodies, the rhythms, and the words to numerous songs (or at least a reasonable approximation), and the accompanying movements, not to mention the concept of naming pitches. Very importantly, he had also reproduced the ritual of positive reinforcement: he warmly congratulated his parents on being able to identify the Do, and they played right along, high-fiving each other.

The following week, when I told some of the other parents about Maxime's "music lesson," many of them told me that their children were also giving them music lessons at home. I asked if the children imitated other things: activities from daily life in their daycare centers, for example. Most of the parents said that happened sometimes — although never to the same extent, or with the same level of precision, that the children replicated their musical lessons at home.

The powerful emotional impact of music sets it apart from many other activities in early life. Children tend to react more intensely to music than to almost any other activity — and in their third year, music can help them develop emotionally and socially, through creative play.

We have all seen children inventing stories, pretending to be daddy or the doctor. What's more, most children at this age are given paper and crayons with which to make their first drawings. We rarely encourage them to do the same thing with music.

Yet when given the opportunity, children will happily and spontaneously invent veritable musical soundtracks. Of course, it might sound like random banging on instruments at this stage — but it isn't random in your toddler's mind!

This musical experimentation helps to develop a child's ability to synchronize with others, and to practice self-control and focus. In this way, music can engage children emotionally while also boosting both their social skills and their creativity in the third year of life. In this vital developmental stage, the child takes her first step toward the infinitely complex phenomenon of musical improvisation, which we will explore in coming chapters.

MUSIC AND EMOTION

Why do children choose to imitate certain people or situations? Because of the emotions they associate with them. Most of us mentally replay — and then spontaneously reproduce — the experiences and situations that have had a strong emotional impact upon us, either positive or negative. Maxime would not be re-creating his music class if the experience had not affected him emotionally.

Live music registers more than other activities with children in the first years because the emotional center of the brain — the limbic system, where music is processed — is already fully functional. In addition, an important study from 2013 found that music uses some of the same brain circuitry involved with our need for pleasure and reward — two systems that are a fundamental part of our *sapiens* survival kit. Put simply, music might not be dessert after dinner, or the tiny tip of our pyramid of needs.* Instead, it may have a role down at the base, with our fundamental physiological requirements for health and fulfillment.

Food and sex, both necessary for survival, trigger the release of a neurotransmitter called oxytocin, commonly known as the "bliss hormone." They make us feel happy. Music, too, is a trigger for the release of oxytocin, and it can create much the same sense of satisfaction in the brain and body as a good meal or requited desire. Music also stimulates the release of dopamine, a neurotransmitter involved in the sensation of pleasure. Between the oxytocin and dopamine that flood our brain when we hear a beautiful song, it's no surprise that music can make us feel so very good!

Science has not only identified many of the hormones and chemical transmitters that our brains create but also determined their exact effects. A frightened child's brain is flooded with cortisol,

---

* The American psychologist Abraham Maslow created what is known as "Maslow's hierarchy of needs" in 1943. The hypothesis is often represented as a five-tier pyramid. From the base up, the needs are: physiological, safety, belonging and love, social needs, and self-actualization.

the "stress" hormone. While her cortisol level is high, the child can barely think straight, let alone learn anything. On the opposite end of the spectrum, the happy child with her oxytocin-dopamine-filled brain is primed to learn. When we are happy, we feel free to experiment, to dare, to take risks and grow.

Little Maxime was giving his parents a music class because the activity made him happy. This emotion is also what allowed him to experiment with the piano, fearlessly, attempting to play the music he heard, and using his imagination to fill in the technical gaps.

This is what I call musical "scribbling" — a musical counterpart to the pretend play that children frequently engage in starting around the third year of their lives. Maxime was creating musically at an age when most parents and educators think this is simply not possible. But in fact, it is one of the most important developmental activities that children can engage in during this phase of their lives — if we give them the opportunity.

MUSICAL "SCRIBBLING"

Any parent or teacher knows how much children love to doodle almost as soon as they can hold a crayon and sit up by themselves. It may be a long while before they produce something even faintly recognizable, but identifiable shapes and figures eventually emerge. As we saw in the previous chapter, language acquisition follows the same curve: from approximation to actual words. And it's the same with music.

If children are not "scribbling" musically, it is usually because no one has given them a chance to do so. One thing I've learned in my more than thirty-five years of experience is that as soon as you put a musical instrument in a child's hands, they will attempt to play it. It doesn't need to be a fancy violin or even a piano; a child can begin making music with a pot and a wooden spoon. Inventing words or stories or melodies while banging on the pot is baby's first improvisation, and it can be a joyful and creative experience.

Many parents today are terrified at the idea of improvising a musical activity because they believe that only trained musicians are capable of improvising even the most basic musical exchange. Sadly, this is yet another example of how we have become utterly blocked regarding our natural ability to make music — especially improvised music. We all improvise every day with words and ideas, in our work and in our kitchens, sometimes even with the truth, but musical improvisation just terrifies people. We need to force ourselves to get out of the rut, sit down on the floor, and start scribbling with music alongside our children.

Raid-the-Kitchen Jam Session

Open your cupboards and take out pots, pans, wooden spoons, and other utensils. You can take out some jars and fill them with different amounts of water; this will add to the variety of sounds you and baby can produce. Take all of this into baby's room, or any place in your home where you can sit comfortably with your child.

Place the whole array of kitchenware on the floor in front of you, each of you sitting on the opposite side of your materials. Now each one of you can take a spoon and begin. Your child may already be banging on everything, which is wonderful, but the idea here is to draw her into a conversation.

You can start by saying and tapping at the same time:

Who is my favorite baby baby baby?

Maybe she will answer you saying "*me,*" or maybe she will repeat "*baby baby baby.*"

Any and all personal subject matter is perfect, and repeated words help her to join in:

I know you love your teddy bear, teddy bear, teddy bear

You can also have fun with gibberish:

Doop baba doo
Woo woo woo
Shabadaba boom boom zip . . .

Then you can move into a purely rhythmic conversation: no words, just a call-and-response piece played out on pots and pans.

You can experiment with your water jars, tapping them with a spoon. Your child will delight in the different sounds. Now you can play the question-and-answer game on your very own glass harmonica!*

---

* *The glass harmonica is a musical instrument made out of glass bowls. Benjamin Franklin invented his own version in 1761 after hearing the haunting sound of wine-glasses being "played." It was most famously used in Mozart's opera* The Magic Flute.

The idea here is to create a musical back-and-forth, much like a verbal conversation. In doing so you are introducing your child to another language — one that she enjoys and excels at as a two-year-old. Of course, after five minutes it's time to go wild and just sing and bang away!

The next level of musical scribbling can include an actual musical instrument, but as we saw with Maxime, it does not require music lessons — nor does it require musically trained parents. I love it when I see children pretending to play the piano long before they have the physical capacity to do so. Often one can identify the music the child is imitating, because it looks and sounds like the skeleton of the actual piece of music that the child has previously heard. (Listening to recorded music might create this desire to improvise, but seeing and hearing people playing live music always has a stronger effect on children. Some parents have told me that their child's first exposure to live music was with street musicians; they describe their child stopping in her tracks and staring, mesmerized by the live musical experience. I love the image, but it also makes me sad to think that so many children must "happen upon" their first exposure to live music rather than being exposed to it more intentionally and more often.)

Over the course of my research for this book, many parents have sent me films of their children "playing" the piano at home. (I use scare quotes upon this first use of the word because truly playing the piano — or any other instrument for that matter — is something that children technically cannot accomplish before the age of five without inappropriately aggressive training.) The videos vary, but often the child is sitting at the piano and caressing the keys while singing. The words to the songs, like the music they are creating just by touching the keys, are deliciously approximate. The children are completely engaged in their musical scribbling, loving it, and can easily remain focused for more than five minutes — a very long time for a two-year-old.

One of the films that a parent shared with me was of two-and-a-half-year-old Émile, who was trying to play the songs he sang in his Baby Musicking class. He began by playing these songs on the family's kitchen table, using his fingers gently, just as if he were playing a real keyboard. When his mother asked what I thought about Santa Claus bringing Émile a piano for Christmas, I said, "Please do, but be prepared!" And indeed, once Émile had his piano, he spent hours in front of the instrument — placing his hands on the keyboard, much like he had seen our pianist do, randomly playing notes while singing the songs from his music classes. His parents are not musicians, but they nonetheless encouraged all of Émile's musical explorations. He was playing and singing, and the result became closer and closer to the actual music!

Far more important than accuracy was the fact that Émile was searching on his own: he was teaching himself. His parents also filmed him playing along with a recording of *The Magic Flute*. Émile would accompany the arias precisely in rhythm with both hands playing on random notes, but when the orchestra came back in for a *tutti* section (when the aria ends and the orchestra takes over), he

lifted his hands and made twirling motions that looked like the full orchestra sounded. With both Maxime and Émile, you could understand perfectly what piece of music they were playing, and if you turned the volume off, they both looked like accomplished pianists.

In developed countries, children rarely have the same opportunity for musical exploration and musical improvisation that they have for language experimentation or other forms of artistic "scribbling." I know very few children who are encouraged to "play" the piano before proper lessons. Even singing songs with children in our homes is becoming rare. This is regrettable because there is a specific window, a period of heightened sensitivity, in which both language and natural aural musicality are acquired organically and definitively. The act of searching for a melody by ear at an early age sets in place a physical relationship with pitch and melody that is much harder to achieve later in life.

What was Émile hearing in his mind when he was playing with the recording? The entire *Magic Flute* opera? On the basis of my experience, I'd argue that the answer is yes.

Late one spring, we had a group of children playing a small part of "Spring" from Vivaldi's *The Four Seasons*. They were a charming orchestra of three-year-olds, holding their tiny violins as best they could, using their bows somewhat haphazardly on an open E string ("open" because the string is not "fingered" on the neck by the left hand) while their teacher played Vivaldi's theme on the piano. The children were nominally accompanying the piano, but most of all they were hearing the entire work and experiencing being a part of the whole, blissfully nonjudgmental about their level of participation.

Later that day, when their parents and caretakers arrived to collect the children, Vivaldi's "Spring" was playing resoundingly on the stereo at the children's request. "Do you hear Vivaldi?" three-year-old Charlotte excitedly asked her mother. "I play it on the violin. I love it!"

Victor Wooten, the Grammy Award–winning American bass guitarist, had much the same experience within his own, very musical family. Wooten was given a two-string guitar at the age of two and encouraged to play along with his older siblings while they rehearsed. Like our budding violinists, little Victor did not hear his tiny two-string guitar; he was hearing the entire piece of music being played by his expert older siblings. The pleasure that Wooten derived from that experience came not from the raw sensation of the music, or any sense of mastery or accomplishment therein, but rather from the sensation of joining an ensemble — feeling the comfort of belonging.

In the same way they learn to speak, children experience and learn music through imitation and experimentation, but also through interaction. These interactions gently teach the child about essential life skills such as self-control, focus, and the ability to anticipate. Why? Because if a child is participating in a musical activity, there is always a precise starting point and an end. There is also, in almost all music, a steady beat. Very few children will voluntarily play out of rhythm, or continue on after the end of the piece. Children understand these unspoken rules and begin to obey them long before their first music lesson.

ARTHUR, KING OF ROAR

Arthur is a two-year-old boy in our Baby Musicking class. Ever since the first time we sang and danced an extract of Camille Saint-Saëns's "Lion King" from *The Carnival of the Animals,* Arthur was in love. All children enjoy this music — especially the part that comes after we sing our made-up lyrics, *"I am the lion king, listen listen to me roar,"* when we all roar in unison. But Arthur seems to enjoy it most of all.

During the song, the children and adults are all on all fours, taking giant lion steps with their front paws. As soon as the piece starts, Arthur opens his mouth and scrunches up his face soundlessly. He stares at the teacher, waiting, eyes open wide. An instant before the word "roar" is pronounced, Arthur lets out a guttural roar unimaginable in a child so small.

The room erupts with laughter and Arthur is beaming. This is the moment he has been waiting for all week, and the waiting itself is what is so remarkable.

Arthur has anticipated the moment when he is allowed to roar in this musical fragment, and he beats the rest of us by a split second. This means that at the age of two, Arthur remembers the piece and its exact musical form and syntax from just one three-minute exposure per week. He anticipates exactly when the roar will come, and he exhibits the self-control necessary to wait for the appropriate moment.

I was curious: Was Arthur following the words or the music? It is almost impossible to take the music out of poetry because the words have rhythm and cadence regardless of whether there is a melody. Yet one can easily take the words out of a piece of music. We decided to do our usual preparation, but at the moment we launched into the refrain, we simply sang "la la la" instead of the words. Arthur still roared right on cue. He didn't need the words; he was following the music.

It is indeed rare to see a two-year-old wait for anything at all, as any parent can attest. And yet, Arthur was willing to wait for the appropriate moment to add his part to the musical construct.

Arthur was spontaneously demonstrating several of the abilities that modern science considers even more important than IQ in determining success and happiness in life: self-control, focus, and anticipation. Music provides the perfect trampoline for the natural development of these abilities.

Without the ability to anticipate, self-regulate, and focus, any musical practice is doomed to sound more like random noise than organized music as we know it. Children prefer synchrony and harmony to cacophony; they instinctively make the necessary adjustments that lessen the chaos and bring forth the music. This occurs because our Western musical traditions contain regular rhythms and predominantly consonant harmonies and melodies. Our children instinctively reproduce Western musical traditions because musical and linguistic enculturation occurs in the first years of life. ("Enculturation" is the scientific word for the way that we absorb not only language but also customs, music, culinary traditions, and even aesthetics.) Children have absorbed a multitude of complex musical codes long before they take their first music lesson — and they use this knowledge instinctively when they begin to make music.

Creating music in a group depends on our ability to anticipate. We need to be able to sense where the music is going and what our musical partners might do next. The need to foresee the immediate future is instinctive; it is part of our autonomic nervous system's lifesaving capacity to react and initiate. The "fight, flight, freeze" response that psychologists talk about has its roots in anticipation.

Learning to clap one's hands at the same time as the rest of the group requires the young child to pay attention to nothing else beyond his own two hands and the musical beat that she is feeling in her body. This is an incredible example of focus!

Musical practice requires this ability to focus, self-regulate, and anticipate. Do children find this difficult? Not at all. They love the feeling of being in sync, and of taking part in something much bigger than the sum of its parts.

PRACTICING SELF-CONTROL — WITH A XYLOPHONE

"Play and Stop" is the instrumental version of "Shake and Stop," which we saw in chapter 2. It is a living illustration of how children learn to concentrate and control themselves through musical play. The children in the classroom are playing xylophones and drums while a teacher begins to slowly sing, "I'm going to . . . play play

play/play play and stop." The purposefully drawn out "I'm going to . . ." requires the children to pay very close attention and anticipate when the downbeat will occur. "Play play play" requires steady beats on the drum or xylophone. "Stop" requires the children to lift their hands in the air and wait until the pianist begins to play again after the abrupt halt.

In the beginning, there is always one child who is not listening or watching, and it is often the other children who ask him to pay attention and stop. It is fascinating to watch a two-year-old asking another two-year-old to pay attention. The reprimand varies from a gentle whisper to the forced removal of the neighbor's mallet with a fierceness only a two-year-old can muster. As the year progresses, the children need less and less help from parents and caregivers with this activity and confidently take charge of their instruments. It is extraordinary when the group gels, and ten two-year-olds start and stop together. The undeniable attraction to being in sync motivates this remarkable coordination of effort.

The children love it when the pianist pretends to go to sleep, making it impossible for them to continue the song. The first time we do this, the children are taken by surprise; they hold their hands and mallets high in the air, barely moving. The room is silent with suspense. This can last as long as seven seconds, an entire day in two-year-old time, before the pianist "wakes up" and begins to play again. The children squeal with laughter and beg for more. Their learning curve is extraordinary. Once they have seen the pianist "go to sleep," we can see them eagerly anticipating the next attack of somnolence. If any of them were not paying attention before, they do so immediately during this game.

This is yet another example of my *highly* scientific formula: laughing child = learning child. As we saw earlier in this chapter, there is actually a chemical basis to this axiom. Amidst their shenanigans, the children are enjoying a musically induced oxytocin high.

Play and Stop with Pots and Pans

I'm going to play play play play play and stop (hands in the air)
play play play play play and stop (hands in the air)
play play play play play and stop (hands in the air)
play play play play play and stop (drop the spoon)

This game can be played with your hands and feet, a pot, and a spoon, or, if you own one, a xylophone or a piano. In this exercise, we will use a pot and spoon. The melody and lyrics are basic, intended merely to set the stage for the development of observation and synchronization.

Chose two pots and two spoons that are size appropriate, making sure that the spoon is easy for your two-year-old to manipulate. Sit down on the floor in front of your child, each of you with an overturned pot between your legs. Raise your hand in the air and begin singing slowly and with suspense, "I'm going to . . . ," then at the word "play," tap your pot vigorously and keep doing so each time you sing "play."

When you get to the word "stop," raise your hand dramatically and hold it suspended in the air. Wait as long as you can, then give a nonverbal cue by raising your spoon slightly to launch the next round. You will most likely raise your eyebrows and inhale without even thinking about it. You will see that your child picks up on these cues and joins you on the "downbeat." These spontaneous nonverbal cues — the raising of your hand or your inhalation — are exactly what a conductor does with his orchestra. These are not special codes for classical musicians. They are universal nonverbal signals that young children quickly learn to imitate. Think of the batter in baseball or even the way we lift a hammer before striking a nail. Split-second careful observation and synchronization are fine-tuned via this simple exercise.

In the beginning, your child will probably keep tapping after the word "stop" — but she'll get the hang of it soon enough. Her desire to be in sync with you will take over, and she will also quickly begin to feel the cycle of seven beats and a silent, hands-in-the-air, suspenseful "stop." The descending melodic line in the last round lets your child know that this is the end, and she gets to drop (or throw) her spoon. Don't be afraid to be silly and pretend to fall asleep. This will only add to the fun. With enough practice, your child will be able to take the lead and you can follow.

One last note: everyone has their own natural tempo — which can change according to our emotional states as well as age. Put simply, this is the speed at which we naturally walk, tap our feet, or clap our hands without an external influence. A child's natural body tempo is about 120 beats per minute on a metronome. Position 60 on a metronome is the same as the seconds on your watch, so 120 is easy to feel: it's two beats per second. The upshot is that if you try to go too slow, your child will not be able to follow.

It is exciting to observe how quickly the children improve, how quickly they learn to move together in synchrony. It feels like there is a magnetic force pulling the children into what I like to call the "orbit of Planet Rhythm." Rhythm functions like a gravitational field; it literally pulls us in and keeps us close — to the shared pulse of the music, and to one another. The two-year-old who waits to roar and the xylophone orchestra that learns to play together are both demonstrating an innate desire to move together in synchrony.

The effects of synchronized movement have been studied abundantly, revealing a great deal about our human potential for empathy and cooperation. Synchronization is one of the fundamental aspects of music that distinguishes it from other artistic activities. When we are in time with one another, when we move together, when we collaborate, we feel a visceral harmony with our fellow people. We become part of the tribe.

THE CHILD WHO LOST HIS MARBLES

There is a significant body of research around synchronized movement and the development of empathy and altruism. In a fast-moving field like neuroscience, in which consensus is rare, the power of rhythm is one of the few things that scientists actually agree upon.

In 2010 Michael Tomasello and Sebastian Kirschner, researchers at the Max Planck Institute in Leipzig, Germany, conducted a fascinating experiment with groups of four-year-olds. They invented two entertaining games to be played by two different groups. Both games were led by enthusiastic teachers, who saw that all the children had plenty of fun. Only one of the games, however, included music and required synchronization among the children. After the activity, the children from both groups were given toys — small tubes containing marbles that made interesting sounds when shaken — and the unsupervised playtime was filmed. The researchers had intentionally booby-trapped one of the tubes; that unlucky child would literally lose his marbles.

The findings were quite clear and, for some, surprising. The children who had participated in the game that included music and synchronization were significantly more helpful toward the marble loser. They would more readily begin to pick up the dropped marbles and attempt to put them back into the unfortunate child's tube. (Interestingly, little girls were even more likely to help than little boys.) The children who had not experienced the musical activity were more likely to carry on playing with their own tubes.

The children in that experiment were four years old, but these tendencies begin much earlier than age four. This was demonstrated, for instance, at Canada's McMaster Institute for Music and Mind in 2014, when director Laurel Trainor and two doctoral students designed an experiment to further explore the psychological effect of rhythmic entrainment in babies. Rhythmic entrainment is a fascinating phenomenon. It occurs in the human body *and* in inanimate objects. In the mid-seventeenth century, the Dutch physicist Christiaan Huygens noticed that the pendulums of his newly invented grandfather clocks began swinging in synchrony when placed near one another. Humans also entrain to one another: drummers seated in a circle may all begin at different tempi (speeds), but they soon start to synchronize with one another, often with no conscious effort.

Trainor wanted to see if sympathetic movement could lead to cooperative behavior not only in four-year-olds but also in much younger children. The subjects of the experiment averaged fourteen months of age. Babies at this age don't yet have the muscle control or coordination to, say, bend their knees in time to specific musical meters, so the researchers needed to find another way to have the babies move in sync with the music.

They decided to bounce the babies. The research team put the babies into strap-on baby carriers in order to do the bouncing. One researcher held a baby facing out in the carrier and stood facing the other researcher. The music began, and everyone started moving up and down in time with the music.

Then the plot thickened; some babies were bounced in synchrony with the person facing them, while others were bounced to a different tempo. Keep in mind that the baby is not seeing the person who is bouncing them; they see only the person facing them.

Next, the babies were brought to another room and placed on the floor in front of the person they had seen while bouncing. In the first scenario, the researcher was pinning dishcloths on a clothesline. She ostentatiously dropped a clothespin and looked at the baby, then back to the clothespin. The babies were given a thirty-second window in which they would either pick up the clothespin and hand it to the researcher, or not.

This part of the experiment was repeated with a variation. In a second scenario, for instance, the researcher was making a drawing, and made a show of dropping her marker. Again, the babies were given a thirty-second window in which to help out, or not.

The results were revealing. Fifty percent of babies who had been bounced in sync with the music brought back the "lost" item as opposed to only 30 percent of the babies bounced out of sync. The in-sync babies also reacted faster.

I find this absolutely incredible. Imagine this fourteen-month-old child: she can barely walk, she is preverbal, and yet she is already capable of altruistic behavior, especially when she feels in sync with another human being — a synchrony facilitated and reinforced by music.

Synchronous movement, like movement of any kind, acts upon our vestibular system — the system in our inner ear that gives us our sense of balance and spatial orientation. Of course, the vestibular system did not evolve specifically for music; rather, it evolved to keep us alive. Yet music stimulates this system in an exquisitely precise manner, as we have seen in chapter 2. Music, via the vestibular system, invites us to dance. And this shared impulse, in turn, brings us closer to one another. We move, we strive to synchronize our movements with others, and we actually feel closer to them as a result and are more willing to be helpful. Quite the virtuous circle.

Synchronous movement is a deep-rooted human phenomenon — but sometimes children do struggle with it. We have never seen an actual case of beat deafness in our school, but we have seen children who have had trouble allowing the vibration or pulsation into their bodies. (If you have ever been to a rock concert, you have certainly "felt" a beat or a pulsation. You feel it in your feet — you feel it with your entire body. When you begin stomping or dancing, this is your body's way of responding to, or *letting in,* this intense vibration. Some children actually struggle to keep out or resist the beat — it can actually frighten them.) We have observed that these same children often lack physical confidence. This suggests that there might be a parallel between allowing a pulsation to enter your body and the confidence necessary to take physical risks.

How to explain these children's struggles? I would argue that the vestibular system is involved, but surely it isn't the only explanation. This is the proverbial chicken-and-egg predicament: Is a child fearful because she cannot trust her body, or is she unconsciously impeding her body's natural abilities out of fear? This is a delicate situation because it is unlikely that a child this age will be able to access the source of her anxiety. There are, however, things that we can do to help children in this predicament.

REACHING OUT THROUGH RHYTHM

Leo was a little boy who could never stay in rhythm with his classmates. Whether the children were clapping, drumming, or dancing, Leo was just . . . off. Although he was too young to verbalize this, Leo — like Elena, the child whose delayed vestibular development I described in chapter 2 — was experiencing what appeared to be that very primal, truly dismal feeling of not being part of the group. Just as Elena had trouble sitting up on her own, Leo was developmentally on par with his classmates except when it came to synchronous movement.

I was concerned that the less capable Leo felt of participating in these rhythmic activities, the more isolated he would feel, which could have negative consequences in other areas of his life. Children who do not notice when they sing out of tune or are out of sync are often carefree, but Leo knew that he was out of sync and was embarrassed about it.

Leo's self-awareness, however, also meant that he could probably learn to get into sync. Unlike carefree children, whose delays are harder to correct because they are blissfully unaware of them, Leo understood that he had a problem. We just needed to find a way to help him.

I decided to try a technique I had discovered in an out-of-print book written by Frances W. Aronoff, a public school music teacher working in New York in the 1960s. Aronoff suggested that if the child cannot match the rhythm or pitch you are creating, you should join them in whatever rhythm or sound they can produce. They may not be able to match your rhythm, but they are definitely aware when you match theirs.

Aronoff was suggesting that, in essence, a parent or educator try reaching out to the child by matching them — building the confidence necessary for the child to be able to make music with others. I have often observed children reveling in the sensation of being in unison and in sync. By creating sound in unison, the two people involved can feel powerfully linked. Two sets of vocal cords vibrating together in unison produce double the sound. But there is more: it is the feeling of vibrating together that is unique. The child who feels his voice joined in precise unison will feel a visceral and powerful connection with the co-singer. The child whose clapping is being matched will experience the sensation of moving together in sync with another human being.

I first proposed that Leo and I play together, just the two of us. I asked Leo to clap whatever he wanted and told him that I was going to be his mirror. Leo's clapping was hesitant to start with, but since the physical effort of clapping is visible, one can actually be in sync with an irregular pulse just by carefully watching the gestures of the person you are clapping with. Almost without being aware, Leo began to relax and find his own natural tempo.

Once the unison is established, the next step would be to move gently toward a regular pulse and then make a small change, and see if the child will follow. I gave Leo a verbal clue to start with, saying, "Okay, Leo, now our train is going to slow down to a full stop." Leo slowed down his clapping with me, and we stopped together. A smile began to form at the corners of his mouth. We then did the opposite: the train went faster and faster. This time Leo burst into laughter. I could see the joy and relief he was feeling.

To ensure that Leo gained enough confidence to be able to relax with his classmates, we continued to do these exercises for a few weeks. To make the transition smoother, we started by playing the same tapping game with the other children, imitating the train slowing down and finally stopping, then going faster and faster. Leo was having the time of his life.

Little by little, we moved into rhythm games that involved not just speeding up or slowing down but actual rhythms layered on top of a steady beat. Leo slowly gained confidence until his differences were gone — and forgotten.

I cannot say with certitude why Leo was not able to spontaneously join in our rhythm games initially, but my intuition is that, in his case, the problem was psychological, not physiological; fear and doubt were stopping him. The thing to remember is that with patience and practice, most young children can overcome what would appear to be a lack of rhythmic ability. The benefits are myriad and profound, and will influence other areas of development, most importantly the child's confidence — but not only that.

THE JOY OF MUSICKING

In the previous chapter, we put the myth of the "Mozart effect" to rest. There's no evidence that music can make you smarter, or better at math or any other skill. When it comes to the development of empathy, however, a positive connection *has* been backed by peer-reviewed, universally accepted scientific research. And yet the race for IQ points is still dominating educational systems in many cultures, in spite of the fact that longitudinal studies have proven that self-control, creativity, and empathy are more essential than IQ to health, happiness, success throughout life. When we make music together, we foster the conditions that make life sustainable and enjoyable. For evidence of this, look no further than any youth choir or orchestra, or any village festival where families sing and dance together.

By their third year, the children at L'École Koenig have "graduated" from their weekly Baby Musicking classes and are now attending our full-day preschool program. By 9:00 a.m. on mornings when the school is in session, most of the children are already in the classrooms enjoying a leisurely moment of free play. Their parents are helping the stragglers take off coats and boots. A few yawns are noticeable — and not only from the children. December days in Paris are short and somber, and everyone has a hard time leaving for school and work in the morning when it's still dark.

In one of the classrooms, our music teacher Matthieu begins playing a short musical motif: *"It's clean up time, nothing more on the floor."* There is an instant change in the atmosphere. The children still in the hallway hurry to hang up their coats and say goodbye to their parents, while the children already in the classroom scurry about, putting away blocks, paper, and crayons. There is no need for insistence from the teachers. None of the teachers has to repeat the instructions or shout, and we don't hear any "hurry ups" from harried parents trying to rush their children into the room. This musical cue tells the children precisely what needs to happen, and they are perfectly happy to clean up, knowing what's coming up next.

Immediately after the "Clean Up" music, the teacher plays our "In a Circle" music. The children rush to form a circle while singing the song; once again, no one has to prod or insist. The implicit rule is that music is the guide. The children smoothly transition from home to school, from outside to inside, from one-on-one play to a group dynamic, all of which happens in record time with much laughter and with no resistance.

The children are very attentive, because if there is too much noise, no one can hear the next musical clue. Indeed, unlike many preschools, we don't need to enforce a listening rule at L'École Koenig, because listening is a necessity that has naturally established itself in our classrooms. Sometimes, however, Matthieu will check to see if the children are paying attention by playing the "Stand Up" music for no reason at all, and then immediately playing the "Sit Down" music, possibly followed by "Crisscross," which prompts the children to fold their legs into a comfortable cross-legged position. Matthieu often pauses halfway through this musical fragment, leaving the children giggling, with their legs half-crossed, stuck high in the air.

Circle time continues with songs from around the world, as well as ear-training games, stomping and clapping, and songs for learning phonetics and math. Sometimes it feels as though the children could learn just about anything if they were doing so within the magic of their musical circle.

This entire morning routine may last only twenty minutes, but it is a beautiful synchronized musical and intellectual workout. As we have seen in this chapter, the synchronization that music requires is an essential prosocial developmental tool. The children move and sing together in a ritual that soothes and comforts them. They learn to belong to their tribe by absorbing its specific social codes through music, language, and movement. This is nothing new. Musical enculturation has been going on for centuries — and has always served the same purpose: the formation of social bonds. Social cohesion is necessary for every society, and music promotes it.

"For there to be an I, there has to be a you." Every one of the scientists I have written about in these first chapters has confirmed this seminal declaration from the philosopher Martin Buber. Buber hypothesized that as a species, we develop a sense of self through our relationship with others. We have a spiritual and physiological need for communication. Only through bonding and social interaction can the mind and psyche develop healthily, allowing our progeny to acquire language, which enables them to understand one another and share their stories via dramatic and musical narrative. We do not learn alone; there is no learning without the essential first duet: I-You.

We know that musical motifs are a more effective means of installing a group dynamic than verbal commands. The musical version of this process involves both the body (the vestibular system) and the emotional mind (the limbic system), and, very importantly, taps into the spontaneous urge to move together created by music. Let's look at one extremely compelling explanation for what's taking place in a child's brain during our circle time every morning.

THE 7 CS

Stefan Koelsch, a researcher in biological psychology and music psychology at the University of Bergen in Norway, is also a talented violinist whose work on the neurological function of music and emotion is extraordinary and should be read by every educator and parent in the world. He's identified seven key social functions, or benefits, of musical engagement — what he calls the "7 Cs." They are as follows:

1. Social contact
2. Social cognition

3. Co-pathy*
4. Communication
5. Coordination of actions
6. Cooperation
7. Social cohesion

As Koelsch puts it when describing the 7 Cs: "The ability, and the need, to engage in these social functions is part of what makes us human, and the emotional effects of engaging in these functions include experiences of reward, fun, joy, and happiness. Exclusion from engaging in these functions has deleterious effects on health and life expectancy."

The 7 Cs are a powerful reminder of how important music is for children's development during the third year of their lives, when they are beginning to find their place not only in their preschool classrooms but also in the giant billions-strong tribe we call humanity. But at a more granular level, the 7 Cs also help to reveal the intricacy and interconnectedness of the developmental processes that children are engaged in when they do something as seemingly simple as sitting in a circle and singing or moving together to music. We see the seven elements of Koelsch's hypothesis enacted in our classrooms every day:

1. Social contact: The children are making music together; they are aware of one another intuitively and viscerally.
2. Social cognition: The children are "interpreting" the suggestions and intentions of their teachers and peers as well as the emotional valence of the songs they sing.
3. Co-pathy: You only need to watch for a few seconds to notice how much the children are experiencing interpersonal bonds; they help and encourage one another continually.
4. Communication: Communication is inherent in music. It is nonverbal, intuitive, and comforting.
5. Coordination of actions: When children move, sing, and

---

* Koelsch's own term for the social version of empathy.

dance together, they do so with synchronization. They learn to adjust, to be in time with one another.

6. Cooperation: The children wait their turn and help one another when needed.

7. Social cohesion: When children participate in a pleasurable musical activity, the group gels; the individuals form a family. The process takes place in the first few weeks of a school year, when children are just getting to know one another. Many of them do not speak French or English, yet all of them speak music together.

I have always loved the humanity of the 7 Cs. It is a precise and compelling scientific explanation of what we see in our schools. Entire classrooms of very young children are listening carefully for musical cues to understand what's coming up next. The benefits are enormous: children learn, feel, develop, and behave better when music is part of their lives. Music is teaching the children to listen and cooperate naturally, with attention, care, and joy.

Sometimes when we have to tell the children that the day is over and they must go home, I am reminded that music is the exception for some of our students rather than the norm. One little girl once told us that she did not want to go home because her mommy did not "know how to music." It broke our hearts. With this book, I hope to ensure that every loving parent feels confident they "know how to music"!

THE MIRACLE OF THE MIND

In the fourth year of your child's life, she will astound you with what she already knows about the world. She has a visceral understanding of things that you made no conscious effort to teach her! She is a creative and emotional powerhouse, and music is her ideal means of expression.

4 YEAR FOUR
Days of Miracle and Wonder

SCAN ME

ONE NOVEMBER I WAS VISITING THE CAMpus of L'École Koenig where our youngest preschoolers attend school. It had been a few weeks since I had seen this group of children, and I was eager to find out how their first experience of school was going. At this point, the children had been in school and musicking daily for three months. I arrived in one of the classrooms just in time for one of the morning circle time rituals: musical roll call. As you saw in chapter 1, each child in our school has a musical name, and when the pianist plays it, the children are encouraged to stand up and say hello or do a little dance.

These children were just turning three, and for children that age, expressing themselves in front of a group can be a challenge. By

November, however, they had come up with some very enthusiastic performances. Martin, who has a very rock-and-roll musical name, does an "Elvis the Pelvis" routine every morning when his name is played. The children love it, and the adults always crack up.

The children enjoy this ritual because they are attracted to the magic of being able to name something invisible. They shout out the names of their peers when they hear the musical motifs and eagerly await their own. If the pianist forgets someone, the children will immediately remind them.

The pianist also "calls" the teachers with their musical names. Normally I can pick out these names easily, just as the children can. But that morning I didn't recognize the musical motif that the pianist played for one teacher's name. What's more, it was surprisingly low and slow.

"It's Marianne, but old," called out three-year-old Ilyes. And so it was: the musical name of one of the school's teachers, Marianne, a sprightly young woman, was slow, low, and frankly ugly. No wonder I didn't recognize it — but how amazing that Ilyes did!

Marianne stood up, hunched over, and lurched a few steps before the pianist "transformed" her by playing the same musical motif faster and higher up on the piano. Everyone sang "Marianne, Marianne," while Marianne began to move like the lively twenty-four-year-old that she was.

The teachers and children seemed to have done all this before, so I asked the teachers afterward how the notion of "old" had come about. They said that it was indeed Ilyes, a bright-eyed, articulate three-year-old, who had first described the low and slow music as being "old." He was accustomed to hearing this musical motif at a fast tempo and played in the middle octaves of the piano. As a joke on Marianne, our pianist played it very low and slow one day. Ilyes said, "It's Marianne but old!" for the first time — but not the last.

The fact that Ilyes could identify the transposed motif was extraordinary on its own. The qualification "old" was a perfect example of transversal thinking. In geometry a transversal is a line that cuts across two or more other lines. What we now call transversal thinking is the ability to use a specific skill set for something new — completely outside the area in which it was acquired. Educators today are aware of the vital importance of developing this ability because on a purely practical level, transversal thinking will help people negotiate exponential change in their lives and jobs.

What we had just seen was a stunning example of transversal thinking: Ilyes identified the musical motif even when almost all of the musical components had been altered; then he applied his extensive three-year-old knowledge of acoustics and the human aging cycle and gave it a label. This association would not have occurred to Ilyes, however, if there had not been physical and acoustic realities involved. Children have small vocal cords, hence their high-pitched voices. Adults have longer and larger vocal cords, hence lower voices, and older people, for the most part, move more slowly than three-year-olds. When Ilyes heard our pianist playing Marianne's musical name slowly, he put all these pieces together in an instant — and a delightful inside joke was born.

Ilyes's example explodes a common misconception about music: that accomplished musicianship is mysterious, daunting, and the result of formal training rather than experience and exposure. In fact, music can be learned by doing rather than by teaching. This is in fact the definition of "musicking"!

Most people imagine musical learning as a pyramid, at the top of which sits the unapproachable complexity of true musical mastery, accessible only to the happy few lucky enough to have been born "gifted" or to have studied classical music for years on end — beginning when they are inappropriately young. This is especially true in economically developed countries where classical music training is put on a pedestal. In an attempt to make their children "musical," many parents will begin enlisting them in formal music lessons around this age, when in fact children are born musical and at this stage are still learning by doing — and doing so entirely happily. Too often, formal training such as classical music lessons will short-circuit this organic process and replace it with something much less enjoyable and effective.

Classical music is certainly one of our greatest cultural achievements, and training in classical music is one of the most demanding and rewarding paths one can choose to follow in life. Gradually over the past few centuries, however, we have lost sight of the oral origins of music — and have needlessly complicated what is actually a very simple and organic process of mastering music.

Sadly, today many children begin their musical lives struggling to learn to read music. This is an example of top-down learning, in which explicit knowledge is taught first, and implicit knowledge follows: students begin by learning concepts, and only eventually get an opportunity to put them into practice. But on the basis of my experience and my research, I confirm that very young children neither respond to nor benefit from top-down music lessons.

As we have seen in previous chapters, musical practice in early life is a sensory and emotional experience. Almost all profound and lasting learning in early life begins with sensory experience. This is bottom-up, age-appropriate learning.

Music is not an abstract, man-made construct; it is rooted in natural physical and acoustical laws. This explains why a three-year-old will make spontaneous, spot-on musical choices long before her first music lesson. Many acoustic and rhythmic phenomena are directly linked to the human body. We have a regular heartbeat, and with our two feet we walk and run at a steady pace. It comes as no surprise therefore that the presence of a steady beat is found in music almost everywhere.

Similarly, our experience of, and response to, high notes and low notes, or "major" or "minor" keys or modalities, is rooted in both enculturation and our sensory apparatus. Children demonstrate this implicit knowledge, and they will gladly share it if we listen and encourage them.

As a species, our learning began with the body and our sensory experience. The same embodied, bottom-up progression can be observed in our children's daily learning processes. It is as if each child experiences an accelerated version of our collective evolution. Delving more deeply into the processes at work in the toddler brain will help parents and educators establish a fun-filled relationship with the building blocks of music — but not only that. Musical experience can be a trampoline for the development of language, physical coordination, and, as we have seen, transversal thinking.

MUSIC AS METAPHOR

The ability to choose the word "old" to define the character represented by a piece of music goes much deeper than music theory or awareness of pitch. No one had taught Ilyes this: his mind had made a spontaneous link between language, music, and the human body. To begin to understand Ilyes's surprisingly accurate use of the word "old," we first need to understand how he could possibly have made the incredible leap between the separate genres of music and language. As adults, we are aware that music and language each possess highly sophisticated structures and vocabularies. And yet, as we have just seen, a three-year-old was able to reach across the divide and qualify a piece of music with a precise word — and his qualification was extraordinary. Many of us will spontaneously say that a particular piece of music makes us feel happy or sad, but the word "old" was in another ballpark altogether. There is an explanation for how a three-year-old could make such a connection, and it is utterly compelling. Musical codifications are linked to the experience of our bodies because high and low in music are acoustic phenomena linked to nature. As we will now discover, high and low in language are also linked to nature and our bodies.

George Lakoff and Mark Johnson, a linguist and a psychologist, respectively, decided in 1979 to tackle the question of whether metaphors might influence how we think. They sat down for what they presumed would be a short investigation into their shared intuition, but instead they remained seated and wrote an entire book in just two weeks. Their *Metaphors We Live By* was published in 1980 and is still considered groundbreaking.

Lakoff and Johnson suggest that metaphors shape the way we

think and are linked to the human body. "Up and down" and "high and low" are the first and most basic examples. Being awake means standing up and sleeping means being horizontal. Being alive requires verticality and movement, being dead is, well, horizontal and motionlessness. The number of metaphors that have come out of these two body states is almost endless.

"I'm feeling down today."

"My income is up by ten percent this year."

"I am a high-minded person."

"He has low self-esteem."

Lakoff and Johnson also concluded that the notions of forward and backward come out of our visual field. Our eyes are looking at what is in front of us and in the direction in which we are walking. Imagine all the metaphors employing the words "backward" and "forward":

"He is so forward-thinking."

"I'm looking forward to the party."

"She is so politically backward."

Lakoff and Johnson conclude that metaphor is not merely a convenient linguistic device; it actually shapes our understanding of the world. Metaphor has become part of our thought process, and its roots begin in the experience of our physical body in time and space. Notions of up and down have evolved from their concrete and physical state into a way of describing moods, feelings, and even time.

Musical pitch, timbre, and rhythm are also products of the human body and its relationship to size, space, and time. Just as a huge man will have a lower voice than a child, a large feline will have a deeper, louder roar than a kitten. Likewise, larger musical instruments have a lower pitch than small ones. Think of the tiny piccolo and the giant double bass. Inside a piano, the short, thin strings on the right produce the "high" notes and the longer, thicker strings on the left produce the "low" notes.

It is very difficult to attribute absolute universality to anything in music, but the use of low sounds in Western music tends to correspond to mystery, fear, and danger. Low-pitched notes feel frightening and menacing and sometimes mournful because our subconscious (autonomic system) associates deep and loud with superior size and danger. Higher-pitched notes, by contrast, often correspond to joyful depictions of nature.

Low and high are also used to illustrate physical size — and classical music is full of literal illustrations of this. In Prokofiev's *Peter and the Wolf*, the bird is incarnated by the flute and the grandfather by the bassoon (literally, "low sound" in French). Similarly, in Saint-Saens's *Carnival of the Animals*, the string bass, the largest instrument in the orchestra, represents the elephant, and once again the flute represents the birds.

The use of high, ethereal instrumental sounds, meanwhile, is often found in works depicting transcendence, as in Gustav Mahler's Ninth Symphony. As he wrote this exquisite composition, Mahler knew that he was dying, and that this would be his last work. The symphony ends with the violins playing so high up, you can no longer distinguish pitches. The music seems to ascend slowly and painfully, and then, before you understand what has happened, the music is no more.

We find the same correspondence of metaphor and the physical world in the technical terms we use in music. This is the case, for instance, with the words "flat" and "sharp." A sharp is a half step higher in pitch, or to the right on a keyboard: we are moving *up*. A flat is a half step lower in pitch on the other side, going lower or *down*. Illustrated on the next page, the words "sharp" and "flat" instantly evoke these phenomena: "sharp" implies something pointy and vertical, whereas "flat" is, well, flat.

Likewise with the familiar musical terms "major" and "minor." These words, which come from Latin, simply indicate size: think of a major event as opposed to a minor event. In technical terms, the difference between a major and a minor chord is determined by the second of their three notes. The distance between the first and second notes is bigger in the major chord.

Of course, most people identify major and minor chords in terms

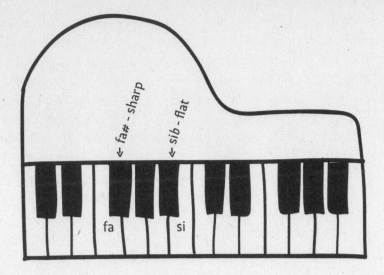

of the emotions they evoke rather than any sense of size. And in fairness, you could say that the sadder mood created by the minor chord is somehow a lessening of the big, proud major chord. (With that said, we need to keep in mind that the associations of happiness with major chords and sadness with minor chords are not universal to all cultures; they are part of our specific Western musical tradition.)

For Western cultures, at least, the distinction between major and minor chords really is that simple — it must be, because we see three-year-olds identify major and minor with ease. At the age of three, Ilyes is demonstrating acute musical sensitivity and apparent expertise in the music and metaphor of his culture. Children spontaneously understand the vocabulary and structures of music because, like metaphor, they stem from the human experience.

Children come to music already equipped with the basic tools they need to understand and enjoy it. As parents and teachers, therefore, we need to avoid bogging children down in note reading and music theory too early in life. Instead, we should encourage all forms of experimentation; this will gently lead to a natural understanding of our musical building blocks. Music is a powerful source of energy that naturally commands attention, engagement, and cooperation. Musicking and speaking both involve the ear, but truly listening to either involves the whole body and mind, not just the ears.

I'M LISTENING . . .

There are different words for "listening" and for "hearing" in every Indo-European language, to distinguish the passive physical process of "hearing" from the cerebrally more complex act of "listening." My favorites are in Italian: *sentire* means "to hear," but also to feel, taste, and smell. The Italian verb *ascoltare* takes the cake: it means "to listen" but also to perform a physical medical examination — the epitome of paying close attention.

Hearing is reflexive and unconscious; we hear in our sleep. Listening, by contrast, implies paying attention and some form of intellectual or emotional engagement. It is *listening* that we are observing when children respond to musical cues and when they make music together.

Between the ages of three and four, listening and the ability to pick up on emotional cues are critical developmental milestones. We may celebrate these abilities less than we do walking and talking, but they are no less significant. The development of an awareness of others and the ability to listen are important indicators of healthy development. Listening with understanding can be the key to conflict resolution and social cooperation on any scale. Luckily we can hone and polish our high-level listening skills through musical practice.

As we saw with the OPERA hypothesis, music and language overlap, but music requires superior aural precision. Emotion creates attention, and attention fosters empathy. Learning to make music together is also learning to listen to others, which leads to the ability to "read" the other person and to anticipate their actions and intentions. This may seem a bit over the top, but not when we remember that a child's auditory and emotional equipment is fully functioning at birth. Helping children learn to listen is like playing with a stacked deck, because children naturally gravitate toward activities they are developmentally ready for. Music is a marvelous tool for developing not only aural precision but also an awareness of emotions and moods and of one another — and children's brains are ripe and ready very early in life.

Musical ear training should ideally take place during the same time frame as early language learning. Children learn to distinguish musical pitches as quickly and efficiently as they learn to name colors, but they are rarely offered the opportunity to do so at an early age. Many universities and music conservatories offer courses in ear training, which most students absolutely dread. The adult musical ear is already formed by the time most people take their first ear-training class, making these skills very difficult to master, and the anxiety most students feel only makes the task harder. The child's ear, still forming and malleable, is much more receptive to this kind of learning.

We know that children's musical capacities develop with practice and interaction precisely in the same way that their vocabulary and syntax develop, but while most of us are aware of the critical period for language acquisition, the parallel information concerning musical development still hasn't made its way from the research labs into the public consciousness. As a result, we fail to take advantage of the critical window in which we can develop these remarkable musical capacities.

Not only are we are missing the opportunity to open the child's musical ear, but also we are missing out on encouraging the most exceptional talent of all — the ability to listen carefully, with engagement and emotion. The advantage of an early start is that music becomes another language for children. The fluency children enjoy becomes a part of their ability to communicate and cooperate with others.

To awaken pitch awareness in very young children, at L'École Koenig we have a fun-filled multimodal process. Musical pitches

— what most people think of as "notes," since musical notes denote a specific pitch — become animals or objects, each with a distinct personality: Do-domino, Sol-sunshine, or the frightening Fa-phantom. Each note has a short, highly recognizable musical motif: Fa has eerie, ghostly music, for example.

We begin to sing Do-Re-Mi-Fa-Sol while moving our bodies up from a squat position to full standing and then back down. This not only feels wonderful but also creates a sense of movement as a group. It's a simple choreography: we are singing and dancing these musical pitches into long-term memory. After the first five notes (Do, Re, Mi, Fa, Sol) are in place vocally and bodily, we can begin mixing them up. We begin with only five notes because of our five fingers; this game will evolve into an exercise at the piano at a later stage. Sometimes the teacher will mime a two-note sequence, Sol-Do: from standing, arms outstretched, to squatting, hands tapping Do-domino on the floor.

It's a musical mystery game. The teacher did not sing the note names. The children must solve the mystery by repeating the choreography, this time singing the note names. They do this immediately, without hesitation; in fact, they begin even before the teacher has finished. Are they all singing exactly on the pitch? No, not at the beginning, but they get there, and very quickly. Even if they cannot yet sing the note on pitch, they recognize it instantly. Then it is the child's turn to mime a sequence for his teacher to "find." They love the idea that perhaps their teacher will *not* be able to solve the puzzle.

These are games that you can easily play at home; all you need is a tiny, inexpensive xylophone and your willingness to learn to listen with your child. For instance, if you would like to try out our musical pitch game, you can do so using the following exercise. You will be surprised not just by your child's ability to learn to recognize musical pitches but by your own as well.

Musical Hide-and-Seek with
Do-Re-Mi-Fa-Sol

For this game, it is very helpful to have a xylophone. It can be the most rudimentary xylophone, but it needs to be pitched correctly. Choose a basic, inexpensive musical instrument rather than a fancy toy.

Before beginning, make sure you have memorized the five musical names and can sing and play them distinctly. As with the musical "Hide-and-Seek" game, you will play the syllables that you sing.

> *Do-domino: fast and jazzy (should sound like doop baba doo)*
> *Re–a rainbow: slow and sweet*
> *Mi-meow: fast, gentle, and repetitive (me me me me me me meow)*
> *Fa-phantom: three loud slow beats*
> *Sol-sunshine: medium tempo and bright*

Sit down with your child and your xylophone. You should both be on the same side of the xylophone so that left to right is the same for both of you. Start with Do and Sol only — the notes farthest apart — so that you can both recognize them easily. Play each note with its specific rhythm while singing the note's musical name, making sure that they sound very different. You will be surprised at how quickly you both learn to identify these two notes. Don't forget to insist on how magical it is to be able to name something invisible!

Once you have both played and sung Do and Sol, ask your child to close her eyes and tell you which of the two notes you have just played. Ask her to do the same for you. Then play them one after the other and ask her to sing them back to you. Remind her that the notes really don't like it when you only *say* their names; they want you to *sing* their names.

When you are both comfortable with these two notes, add the Fa-phantom.

When you and your child can easily and consistently identify all three, add the Mi-meow, and lastly the Re–a rainbow.

You do not need to spend more than five minutes a day on this exercise, but the more often you play the game, the deeper the musical memory that you will create. And that is what this exercise is all about: you and your child are creating implicit memories for musical pitch. An implicit memory is an effortless memory. The most famous example of implicit memory is our ability to ride a bicycle. You don't have to search or ponder; it is just there. With implicit musical memory, pitch recognition can literally be at your fingertips. When children have experienced this kind of musical training, they can hear a melody and go to a keyboard and play it — effortlessly.

When professional musicians come to visit the classroom, they tell me that they don't quite believe what they have just seen. They think that this particular group of children must be exceptional. We tell them no, nothing of the sort. This is simply the result obtained when children are given the opportunity to *make* music during the age-appropriate period. The students don't go through any intensive training, and we certainly don't pretend to have a roomful of children with perfect pitch. This skill, whose scientific definition is "the ability to identify or produce the pitch of a sound without any reference point," is said to exist in only one person in ten thousand. Yet recognizing the notes of a melody is apparently natural for young children when they do so daily. Otherwise we would not see the majority of them acquiring this skill so effortlessly — or using it to such extraordinary ends.

KAZUMA THE TRICKSTER

Kazuma was a precocious three-and-a-half-year-old enrolled in our full-time preschool program. His communication skills had been coming along, but socializing was still tricky because of the language barrier: his native language was Japanese, and he was just learning both French and English. What we lacked in linguistic common ground, however, we made up for with music.

At L'École Koenig, one of our children's favorite musical games is verifying if their teacher has superpowers. We use a xylophone for the youngest children; the older ones can go to the piano. Each child gets to test his teacher's powers by playing a note for them to identify with their back turned. In this way we are also reinforcing the children's pitch perception.

One morning our music teacher Alice was playing the magic powers game with her class. It was Kazuma's turn to play a note and ask Alice to identify it with her back turned. He played a Sol, and she sang Sol, keeping her back turned to the class. Kazuma giggled and said, "No, Fa." I suppressed my own giggle and restrained myself from intervening, because it was, in fact, a Sol. He was playing a trick on his teacher. But I needed to know for sure if Kazuma was purposely trying to fool his teacher, or if he truly didn't recognize the note he'd played.

"Oh, let's give it another go. This time can I try?" I said. I gave a conspiratorial wink to Alice; I could see that she had also suspected what Kazuma was up to. I turned my back, and Kazuma played another note. It was Re, so I sang "Re." Again, Kazuma said, "No, Do." He was practically doubled over with laughter. I think he understood that we knew what he was up to, but instead of reprimanding him, we encouraged him. We played the game several more times, and each time Kazuma lied about the note name, and we feigned surprise.

Then we asked Kazuma to turn his back and name a pitch. Kazuma correctly named not one but five different notes instantly.

Kazuma was playing with the truth, and the vehicle for his game was a complete abstraction, a musical pitch. Kazuma, however, did not experience musical pitches as an abstraction; to him they are like people, they are recognizable, they have personalities and even names. His little prank went beyond pitch identification. Kazuma was so sure of his ability to give a name to a sound, so confident in his musical mastery, that he could transform the original game into a highly complex social exchange.

For Kazuma, the superpowers game allowed him to get past the limitations of his rudimentary French language skills and enter into a very intricate communication involving humor and risk taking. It was no longer about being right or wrong about a musical pitch; rather, it was about using his implicit aural skills to tease his teacher, to engage with her in play. He was so confident of his ability to "speak" music that he could play a practical joke on his teacher, at the age of three and a half, without even sharing a common language. Music allowed Kazuma to make a quantum leap toward communication.

THEORY OF MIND

In addition to using his rudimentary knowledge of musical pitches to communicate with his teachers, Kazuma was also demonstrating a developmental skill that is considered one of the important phases on the scale of theory of mind (ToM): the ability to play with the truth — in other words, to lie.

Learning to lie is a natural part of healthy development, and recent research is indicating that it is a sign of intelligence. And it is no wonder that Kazuma was flexing his newfound fibbing muscles in his fourth year of life. Although the foundation for ToM is laid many months earlier — around the middle of the second year, when children learn that, in the words of one researcher, "their own mental states are distinct from those of others" — children typically develop theory of mind between the ages of three and four. In my experience, music can help children reach this major developmental milestone, like so many others.

What exactly is theory of mind? A commonly agreed-upon definition is that it is the understanding of the mental states of others, including their intentions, desires, beliefs, and emotions. It refers to the uniquely human ability to imagine what someone else is thinking or feeling. Since we cannot see into one another's minds, we can only have a "theory" about what might be going on in there. Theory of mind is essential for living together in society.

Although the term was coined only in 1978, notions of intuition or empathy or other variations on this theme have been explored as long as people have been studying human nature. We now understand the rational importance of this identifiable cognitive skill. We also recognize that the lack of this ability is a developmental red flag. Children on the autism spectrum, for example, have difficulty with theory of mind. ToM is not the same as IQ. A child with a very high IQ can still struggle with ToM and have difficulty socializing or connecting with others. Theory of mind is about our uniquely human need to understand one another's desires and intentions. Making music together requires careful attention, observation, and intuition about others, and so can be quite revelatory regarding theory of mind. There is not yet enough research on this subject, but in my thirty-five years of experience, I can confirm that children who display high-level musical sensitivity also demonstrate an above-average ability to read others' emotions. The opposite correlation is also consistent.

Among the stages of theory of mind development is *simulation,* or "pretending to be." Most children love pretend play; Maxime — the two-and-a-half-year-old whose home music class we saw at the beginning of chapter 3 — is a perfect example. Simulation of this sort is a step up from imitation, in that it involves not only consciousness but also intention and emotion. When Maxime replicated our musical games with his parents, he was not just reproducing the musical material from his class. He was intentionally simulating his teacher's emotional expression and intentions; he was in a sense pretending to be his teacher for the duration of his music lesson. This act of "stepping into another's shoes" is one of the developmental stages of ToM. We start by mimicking other people, and in doing so, we learn to sense what they are thinking and feeling.

Music can support and enhance the development of this uniquely human ability. To judge by the number of children in our school who are re-creating their music classes at home, music appears to invite more observation and more simulation than the other activities the children experience at school. But the very act of making music together also requires an attunement to the other person's mind — attention that, in turn, sharpens a student's sensitivity in this regard.

Think about what making music together requires. When I am playing with you, I need to be observing you carefully, so that not only are we in sync rhythmically, but also our intentions match. We cannot produce music together if one of us is creating a bombastic march and the other a quiet meditation. Matching another person's rhythm or musical style may seem too sophisticated or difficult for children, but they are experts at blending their musical moods with those of their classmates — and they do so spontaneously. It is compelling to observe this ability in young children, knowing that it can lead to deep, harmonious cooperation.

THE RHYTHM CIRCLE

The ability to synchronize rhythmically with others is a defining factor in children's early development, as we've seen in previous chapters. When children struggle with rhythm, it can point to deeper challenges: developmental disorders such as dyslexia, ADHD (attention deficit hyperactivity disorder), and ASD (autism spectrum disorder) all share the common denominator of weak rhythm skills. This said, children reach developmental bench marks within a very elastic time frame. There is no reason to panic if your three-year-old cannot yet clap in sync with her friends. The reason that parents and educators should be on the lookout for children who are struggling with synchronizing their movements with others is simply because there are so many ways to support them in developing this skill and all of the attendant cognitive and emotional advantages that come with it.

Between the ages of three and four, most children begin to enjoy moving in synchrony with one another. This is part of their burgeoning social development as well as their biological need to move for vestibular development. We can and should capitalize on this desire because, like pitch, rhythmic expertise can be developed before the age of seven, and the knowledge becomes part of our implicit memory. As with musical pitches, children who experience rhythm first through their bodies will recall the physical sensation when they later use rhythmic notation. They won't have to think about it; their rhythmic ability will be automatic.

The process for early rhythmic training is much the same as for learning pitches: body first. Rhythm is natural for almost all children. They are at ease tapping or stomping out any rhythm. When you ask them to go faster or slower, they respond effortlessly. Rhythm is linked with proportion. Twice as long, half as long, twice as fast: these are all notions that children understand first with their bodies.

When they have mastered the feeling of short and long, fast and slow, we begin using the actual names of the rhythms. In French the "name" of the short-short-long rhythm we have seen previously is *"croche-croche-noire."* The entire "We will, we will rock you" in French rhythm vocabulary is *"noire-noire-noire-noire croche-croche — croche croche —."* While the note names Do, Re, Mi are understood all over the world, the names of rhythms are different in almost every language. Let's take the example of the quarter note. German is close with *Viertelnote* (*vier* is "four" in German). In French it is a *noire,* which means "black"; in British English it is a "crotchet"; and in Italian a *semiminima.* Thankfully, no matter what you *call* them, the graphic systems for both rhythm and melody are the same all over the world.

Once the children can consistently name the rhythm they hear, we then show them what the rhythm looks like in musical notation. We do this using cardboard circles and popsicle sticks, which are easy to manipulate. This is like playing with building blocks — the children are building rhythms.

We know that the children have made the jump from aural to visual recognition (reading) when they can construct a short rhythm segment for their friends with the circles and sticks. This knowledge becomes embedded in both their motor and visual memory. They easily retain the graphic symbols of rhythms because they first experienced the rhythm in their bodies. This is the same process used in the pitch recognition games. The end result in both cases is the ease and pleasure of effortless musical memory. We need to keep in mind that this is precisely what is happening simultaneously with your child's language skills. At three years old she is waxing poetic about everything from the Snow Queen to her passion for purple. She is manipulating both syntax and vocabulary with the greatest of ease because of the robustness of her implicit language skills. After more than thirty-five years of experience, I can guarantee you that children also develop effortless musical skills simply by engaging in the activities described in this book.

The goal of this training is not musical brilliance. Rather, moving together creates social cohesion, which should be a paramount objective for all parents and educators at this stage. Synchronizing our movements, matching our intentions, and reading the emotional states of others are requirements of both music and theory of mind. Proficiency in both is a long process, but it can begin very early with extraordinary benefits. When rhythmic training begins before the age of seven, it can also serve as preventative medicine. Little Leo in chapter 3 — the child who was struggling to stay in sync with his classmates — was brought out of isolation and into belonging thanks to rhythmic entrainment.

Rhythmic practice with groups of children is invigorating and spontaneous. It usually begins with moving to rhythms in a circle — a very powerful experience, and most likely one of our ancestral practices. These rhythm circles were humanity's first orchestras. Music therapists have known this for a very long time, but this knowledge has not yet reached into our parenting and education systems. After you learn more about them, I hope they will become a regular part of your life with your three-year-old, just as they are in our preschool.

Imagine a classroom of three-year-olds seated together in a circle, as their teacher gets them very excited about the story he is going to tell. The story is very dramatic and involves a dark forest and a mysterious and spooky woodsperson. The teacher asks the children to join him in rocking from right to left to a steady beat. (He needs the children to have their hands free and their lower bodies moving to a fixed rhythm; hence the rocking from side to side.) The beat never stops during the entirety of this musical game. Rhythmic entrainment works its magic: the children are moving together as one.

The teacher begins to tell the story beginning with "the whole note" — a musical note that lasts for four beats in 4/4 time, and which therefore takes up an entire measure. In Western music, 4/4 time, or four beats per measure, is a very common rhythm organization, which is why it forms the basis for this game. The whole note is the only note that does not have a stem in musical notation — or as we say, an arm or a leg. This fact, too, is a fundamental part of the game that's now beginning.

ro-o-on-de   blan-che   noire   croche-croche
whole note   half note   quarter note   eighth notes

In the story, the innocent whole note is happily rolling through the woods. It can only roll because it has neither arms nor legs. As the teacher describes the whole note rolling along, the students — still rocking from side to side — sing *"ro-o-on-de,"* moving their hands in a large circle. The *ronde* is, of course, a circle. It's the French word meaning "whole note." Even if you don't know a single other word in French, I would encourage you to remember this one and a handful of others that I will introduce in the pages to come, since they are extremely helpful for music games such as this one.

As we have seen, in different countries, rhythms are called by different names, even if they are always written the same way. French rhythm vocabulary, unlike the American system, is not based on math. The system labels the rhythms by color and shape, both of which are more accessible for young children than mathematical fractions. This may seem illogical, but it actually makes it easy for young children to name the rhythmic elements. Naming a rhythm is most meaningful when the name conjures the feeling. We will see later in this chapter just how close language and rhythm are, but for now, back to the woods.

As the beat continues, the teacher encourages the children to roll backwards in a little ball, coming back to a sitting position on the count of four. The teacher is a human metronome, and the children allow the beat to regulate their movements. Their favorite moment is when one of their classmates does not manage to roll back up and instead rolls to the side. "Oh no, we've lost a *ronde*," cries the teacher. The giggles begin, and of course all the children start rolling around the room.

Then the drama begins: the nasty woodsperson is stalking the hapless *ronde*. He sneaks up from behind and "Bam!" The children make the dramatic gesture of chopping the *ronde* in two. The children hold up both hands, making little circles with their thumb and index fingers (the remaining fingers pointed upwards make the stem) while singing *"blan-che"* (half note) and "one-two." A half note is two beats, or a half measure, and is called *blanche* in French

— "white" — because it is represented by an open circle with a stem. The most important thing is that the children feel that a whole has been divided in two. The steady beat has never stopped; it is a heartbeat or *ostinato* underlying all of the movement and singing.

Once the half note is well understood, the teacher announces the arrival of the wicked woodsperson again. The children are ready, and at the count of four, they make the chopping gesture, again shouting, "Bam!" They hold up both hands with their index and middle fingers extended, singing "one-two-three-four," *noire-noire-noire-noire:* the name of the quarter note in French is *noire* (black), noted as a filled-in circle with a stem.

Imagine if you did this every day for a few months. The sound of the words *ronde* and *blanche* and *noire* would create a spontaneous reaction in your body: you would want to roll backwards and forwards while counting to four or form a circle with your thumb and index finger, or show four quarter notes by showing two fingers on each hand. It will likely become automatic — an implicit memory.

The story keeps going — all the way up to sixteenth notes for the older children, and they ask for it every day. Later they will transfer this physical knowledge to reading rhythms. "Reading a rhythm," however, is almost a contradiction in terms. Although we are *looking* at the graphic representations, when we say that we are "reading a rhythm," we are actually hearing, singing, or playing what we see. The little collection of circles and lines translates instantly into something exhilarating like Ravel's *Boléro* — one of the most popular pieces of classical music in the world. The *Boléro* contains *one* six-beat rhythm segment repeated over and over for thirty-two minutes, and we never want it to stop! It is a question of matching an image to a feeling. When the sensation is intense and experienced in the body, memorization is easy.

WHEN THE BEAT GETS LOST

By now we've seen how important rhythmic practice can be in fostering social cohesion and supporting musical memory. But as I've suggested, there is also a connection between beat perception (feeling an external pulsation) and language acquisition — a connection that we often don't appreciate until we realize that the child is having a problem with either or both of these developmental processes.

In the past, we didn't attribute much importance to whether a child was clapping his hands or marching in time with his classmates; if he was not, he simply was labeled "awkward" or "unmusical," and the beat went on. But now we know that these sorts of issues should be taken seriously, and addressed to the extent that they can be, because they are signs of deeper challenges.

For most people, the ability to tap their fingers and feet in time with music they enjoy is effortless, but for others it can seem like an impossible task. Our young student Leo, from the last chapter, was very fortunate that his difficulty with rhythm was psychological in nature and could be addressed, but we now know that when this ability is missing, it may be an indication of other developmental difficulties.

Sadly, the research on this subject has not trickled down into schools and homes. Many children could be helped early on if their parents and teachers were more aware of what to watch out for. If parents and educators better understood the importance of learning to feel a beat and move together in rhythm early in life, these small problems might never become big problems.

What is certain is that we move our bodies to a beat without much thought or effort because our audio and motor systems work closely together; they don't require much attention from our conscious minds. But when these sensorimotor connections are impaired or not finely tuned, a child will have difficulty feeling a musical pulsation, and other developmental problems may appear. It is impossible to say that the origin of these problems is a deficit in beat perception, but as I've mentioned, science has found a common denominator in children with dyslexia, ASD, and ADHD. These children all have difficulty with beat perception. Often these are the children who can't clap together with the group, or who seem to have two left feet.

During the child's fourth year, spoken language skills are generally soaring. Learning to speak depends, of course, on hearing. Most three-year-olds can pick out rhyming words and even tell you how many syllables they hear — just like they can perfectly sing or tap a short rhythm segment back to you. Research has determined that the child who cannot feel a beat and synchronize may also struggle with the rhythms and cues of spoken language. One of the signs of missing the cues is when the child has a hard time differentiating between phonemes. For example, when asked if the sound of *b* and *d* are the same or different, the child cannot say. These children will also have difficulty noticing rhyming words and separating words into syllables. Think of how basic the ability to tap in rhythm is for most people. It is probably the musical ability that we most often take for granted. This basic sensory awareness is what allows us to move with one another to accomplish everything from synchronized stone heaving to creating multilayered orchestral masterpieces. In this case, when the most basic requirement for joint music making is impaired (the ability to follow a beat and synchronize with another person), another basic human need will be affected: our ability to communicate. But just as music can highlight the problem, it also can contain the solution.

MARCHING TO THE SAME DRUMMER

I am especially interested in the relationship between rhythm and dyslexia because I suffer from a minor form of the syndrome. As a small child, I found that the different spellings of "weather" and "whether" or "there" and "their" were a great mystery to me. I remember thinking, "Why is spelling so important?" and "How could someone not understand the word just from the context?"

When I was eight years old, the children in my elementary school were given a battery of tests. When my scores came back, they were all in the extremely high range, except for spelling, which was at the exact opposite end of the scale. The head of the school, my teacher, and my parents discussed this and agreed that it must have been an error. I'm not sure that any of them had even heard of dyslexia back then.

In high school I belonged to the school band, which became a marching band in the fall and spring, and that meant enduring a grueling practice every morning. The band director, Mr. Hoffman, was very encouraging about my musical talent — until I got out on the marching field. I had an absolutely miserable time trying to play and march at the same time, and Mr. Hoffman would single me out for humiliating scoldings. When my parents noticed that I was increasingly reluctant to go to band practice, I told them the truth. They met with Mr. Hoffman, who showed them the films of band practice. There it was: the marching band members looked like little toy soldiers from high up in the bleachers, except for one soldier who was, well, marching to a different drummer.

Dyslexia can so easily go undetected if no one is looking for the red flags. If anyone had understood that my inability to march to the beat was a basic beat detection problem, this issue could have been addressed early on, sparing me years of spelling uncertainty. Sadly, no one had the slightest idea that there might be a link between the two.

Today I know that I am not alone. So many dyslexics have endured years of humiliation and disgrace in school. Like theory of mind and certain other cognitive disabilities, dyslexia has absolutely no bearing on a person's intelligence — yet how many dyslexics have been treated like the class idiot? How many children have not received the help they needed? This is especially painful to contemplate when you consider that dyslexia has been a subject of debate for more than a century. The study of this condition began in Germany in 1887, and it was first referred to aptly as *Wortblindheit* (word-blindness). As education and literacy rates rose in Europe and the United States, so did the diagnosis of reading problems. Many people continued to doubt the validity of dyslexia well into the latter part of the twentieth century. It was often dismissed as a pseudo-medical diagnosis invoked by middle-class parents to explain their children's poor performance in reading. Although the research of the past two decades has dispelled this myth, public policy in Europe and the United States has only recently recognized dyslexia as a genuine disability.

The fact is that reading is a relatively recent invention in the expansive timeline of human evolution. Human beings have been reading for a mere five thousand years, compared to the 100,000 or more years we've had spoken language. Since reading is an adaptation of spoken language, we need first to understand how spoken language evolved alongside music. Only then can we understand the relationship between reading and music. Spoken language is sound; music is sound. In fact, the root *phon-*, which we find in *phoneme, phonological,* or *telephone,* is from the ancient Greek word for "sound." The brain circuitry and vocal apparatus used for the production of cries and early vocalizations — our first musical productions — may have served as a trampoline for language development.

So in order of appearance, we have cries and vocalization (possibly musical), then language, and then, much later, the translation of spoken language into human-made alphabets. I fear that we often forget this evolutionary order and therefore fail to understand that reading came out of spoken language, hence sound, hence music. One salient example of our oversight is our continued use of "Twinkle, Twinkle, Little Star" to teach children to memorize the Roman alphabet. Usually, using songs to help children learn things is not only enjoyable but also highly effective. But this song teaches the child the letters' *names,* not their *sounds,* and this does not help the child with reading. This misunderstanding persists. Many parents tell me with pride that their child is ready for reading because she has memorized the alphabet, meaning the letters' names. Think of how we could minimize reading difficulties if we recognized that reading comes from spoken language and music — and incorporate this in early reading programs.

To further grasp this idea, let's look at the common denominators: both speaking and musical production involve rhythms, patterns, audio perception, and motor skills. These are part of the over-lap in Patel's OPERA hypothesis. And this is why, when a child has a reading or speech difficulty, musical interventions can be a solution.

In a fascinating study run at the University of Cambridge in 2002, three groups of children — a group of dyslexic children, a control group of non-dyslexic children, and a group of children who had learned to read exceptionally early — were tested for phonetic and rhythmic sensitivity. One of the tests involved their ability to hear basic "amplitude modulations" (or beats) in sound waves. Rhythm in speech is made up of these slow amplitude modulations and corresponds roughly to the sound modulations found in phonemes or single syllables. By pronouncing these syllables out loud, most of us can distinguish the percussive quality of *pa* from the gentler *ma*.

This distinction is difficult for dyslexic children to make; they just do not hear or feel the difference. The ability to make this distinction is what allows a child to begin to identify syllables in a word and separate words in a sentence. This leads naturally to increased comprehension. This ability is shown to be in direct correlation with the ability to synchronize to a beat.

The Cambridge study found a direct correlation between basic auditory processing ability and differing degrees of literacy. The weakest beat detection was found among the dyslexic children; the highest level of beat detection belonged to the early readers. Children who were neither early nor late readers also showed beat detection in the middle range. This was one of the first studies that spotted the correlation between poor rhythm skills and substandard reading ability. We now have studies proving the efficacy of music therapy, especially rhythm therapy, in overcoming these difficulties.

Music practice for very young children can serve as both an early detection system and a developmental boost, and might just save some families the high financial and emotional costs of remedial reading programs, psychotherapy, and special needs classes. Early intervention could be as easy as clapping together with your toddler — or chanting nursery rhymes.

THE MAGIC OF NURSERY RHYMES

Usha Goswami, who led the 2002 Cambridge study, has had a distinguished career studying developmental dyslexia and beat perception. She is a great proponent of the use of nursery rhymes and clapping games in early childhood. When we take a close look at the standard nursery rhyme format, it reads like the result of twenty years of neuroscientific research into language acquisition. All the ingredients are there: Nursery rhymes are short — four to six sentences long — and they have a predictable rhyming pattern and a catchy, repetitive rhythmic composition. They often involve hand-clapping or even more elaborate movements, and they are alternately nonsensical, funny, and dark. As a result, not surprisingly, they act as a magnet for children's attention, and yet most of them date from the sixteenth and seventeenth centuries. The first nursery rhymes may have been lullabies, and the first recorded example of what we would later call a nursery rhyme was "Pat-a-Cake, Pat-a-Cake, Baker's Man," which appeared in a play by the British playwright Thomas d'Urfey in 1698.

We all have our favorite nursery rhymes, which today have become synonymous with Mother Goose rhymes. (Mrs. Goose was actually a fictional character created by the seventeenth-century French fairy-tale master Charles Perrault.) The format of classic nursery rhymes such as "Humpty Dumpty" or "Three Blind Mice" is essentially musical, and their success and longevity lie in their repetitiveness, "rhythmicness," and predictability — as well as their entertaining subject matter, of course. Many of them are actually thinly disguised horror stories!

But in some ways, nursery rhymes have been a victim of their own success. More than three hundred years since its creation, this incredible tool for language learning has barely been updated. You can make your own family nursery rhymes, however; indeed, these could be the ones that your children will remember forever.

Your Very Own Nursery Rhyme

You need three ingredients:

- two sets of rhyming words
- a catchy rhythm
- a simple subject, preferably slightly dramatic and impera-
tively one that involves your child

For the rhymes, how about "balloon/soon" and "stay/day"?
For the catchy rhythm, let's borrow from "Humpty
Dumpty":

My daughter's name is Elsa, and as a baby, she was quite the
daredevil. This was what I came up with, and I promise it did not
take days . . .

Elsa loves her bright red balloon
Elsa plans to fly away soon

Next, we add a little excitement and rhythmic acceleration:

All of her friends beg her to stay saying
Please Elsa fly away some other day!

Think of all the gestures you can make and the laughter you will share with this last couplet!

Knights and ogres and fairy godmothers might be intriguing,

but at this stage your child is probably more interested in people and experiences from her own life. By following this simple
recipe and adding the magic ingredient of personalization, you
are feeding linguistic superfood to your child. She will love every minute and beg for more.

We would never dream of asking a child to learn to read a nursery
rhyme before they had danced and clapped it over and over. Thankfully, nursery rhymes have remained an oral tradition, as well they
should.

ORAL TRADITIONS

There are still places in the world where music has remained an
entirely oral tradition; no one learns to read music at *any* age. Indian classical music contains some of the most highly complex melodic and rhythmic systems on the planet, and yet there is no written form. Children in India begin learning rhythmic sequences very
early with a system called *teentaal*. These are spoken syllables that
help reinforce memorization of the complex rhythmic sequences.
They sing melodies with the Hindustani equivalent of Latin note
names: Sa Re Ga Ma Pa Da Ni Sa.

This is yet another vivid example of musical and linguistic hand-
holding. Indian master musicians don't read music, yet they use
syllables for memorization just like Westerners. A major difference
between classical music from India and Western music is that Hindustani music, while highly codified, is primarily improvisational.
When you hear the word "raga," perhaps you imagine a lengthy musical score. There is no score; there is only a specific scale, and a
mutually agreed-upon structure. Early, entirely aural training allows Hindustani master musicians to both adhere to structure and
be very free.

I had a telling experience while performing in India with my Indian guru and friend Deobrat Mishra. It was very humid, and one of the keys on my flute got stuck. In the midst of my improvisation, a note came out a half step flat. This was a tiny anomaly, a single note, a split second of sound, but Debu looked at me as though I had just committed high treason. Debu never learned to read music, but this one fleeting "wrong note" in the middle of a complex piece of unwritten music instantly caught his attention. He is no less a musical expert because he does not read music.

Music in India, as in many non-Western countries, is still linked to family traditions. Children in musical families begin their initiation very early, and entirely orally. This is a reflection of music's integral role in family and community life in these nations.

This model doesn't exist any longer in the European world where I live, but it could and it should. We can immerse our children in music early, and once they are fluent, we can show them how to make a record of their musical experience, as well as how to absorb the music created by others. The spatially oriented Western system of musical notation makes this possible, and even has an advantage over Indo-European alphabets because it actually looks like it sounds. Melodies move up and down in pitch and on the staff as well. Rhythms are fast and close together or stretched out and slow. In fact, a musical score has always looked more like a map than a book to me.

Mozart : A Little Night Music

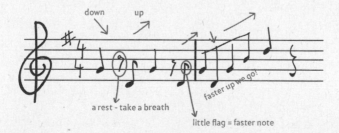

At a later stage in their musical experience, generally around the age of six or seven, children will understand that musical notation is just a shortcut to more and more music. Of course, this is exactly how we go from speaking to reading and writing. We encourage speaking in the youngest children, until their speech seems fluent and effortless, and then we introduce reading and writing. So too with music: once children can "speak" it, they understand what they stand to gain by learning to read it, and eventually to write it. But in the fourth year of life, children need to sing and dance together — they need to invent implausible stories with wonderfully approximate musical soundtracks.

PLAYFUL LEARNING

As children's language skills fall into place between the ages of three and four, we can begin to see their first playful make-believe stories coming to life. This is a natural outgrowth of our desire to create and share the narratives of our lives. But it is only the beginning of children's creative journeys. As they take their next amazing steps in musical scribbling, children will invent entire musical stories, with virtually no instrumental training. As we've seen, children are able to tap into musical universals such as high and low, safe or scary, with no instruction. Next, we will see where children take these innate abilities during the fifth year of life — and how this child-motivated playful learning is linked to the creative problem-solving skills that twenty-first-century education specialists are encouraging in schools everywhere.

5 YEAR FIVE
Rationality and Unicorns

SCAN ME

FOUR-YEAR-OLDS GET EXCITED WHEN LEARN-ing about the world and its history — provided you can bring these abstract topics to life for them and help them to connect these subjects to their own lives. If you want preschoolers to understand the importance of Mahatma Gandhi, bring him into the classroom, literally.

At our school, we invite actors to inhabit the roles of historical figures and come play with the children. Mozart has visited; he regaled the children by sitting on the floor and playing the piano blindfolded. Potemkin frightened them a bit, but Salvador Dalí was a hit, making his entrance on a bicycle that he said was his wife. Marie Antoinette taught the children how to bow and curtsy, and explained that the life of royals was not always rosy. (We carefully avoided any reference to her gruesome demise.)

A breathless silence takes hold of the children when a costumed character walks into the classroom. At four years old, your child may be well spoken and logical, but she probably still believes in unicorns. Their open-mindedness and capacity for wonderment at this age — plus their well-honed motor skills, linguistic abilities, and theory of mind — make children's fifth year an extraordinarily creative time. When they have a foundation of musical experience to build on, their creative output will not be limited to painting and pottery. Children will create musical stories and soundtracks because for them, music is just another means of self-expression.

When I invited William Shakespeare to come and discuss his writing with the children, they set about preparing to present to him a little opera I wrote, based on three Shakespeare plays, with appropriate Elizabethan music. As the children sang and beat their drums to the invigorating "To be or not to be" song, Shakespeare entered, dressed in full sixteenth-century regalia. The children looked simultaneously enthralled and overwhelmed. He bid the children good morning, and they replied timidly. But when Shakespeare asked them if they knew who he was, they finally relaxed, pleased to share their extensive knowledge of his plays and characters.

Shakespeare stifled a grin as he listened to the students' four-year-old interpretations of some very complex emotions and ideas. The children tried to explain to him why Romeo could not marry Juliet because their families did not get along. It was a bit confusing, but Shakespeare knowingly rubbed his chin and said, "Yes, such a tragedy . . ." They then told him how a magic potion had made Titania fall in love with a donkey; he began galloping about the room braying loudly, to their absolute delight. Our actor, who loved the physicality of live theater, then told the children that he was going to show them what acting, or make-believe, is all about.

Shakespeare launched into a thrilling scene about a ship at sea in the midst of a terrible storm. He threw himself into the performance, becoming the wind and the waves, working in a steady crescendo, swirling his cape, roaring, and moaning. I accompanied him, improvising a musical storm on the piano. Suddenly, we were all on the ship with Shakespeare.

At the peak of the storm, he soared to the sky, then crashed and crumpled onto the carpet, uttering one last heart-wrenching moan. The sudden silence was total. The children were rapt, having wholly entered the world of make-believe. Unfortunately, they now believed that Shakespeare was dead.

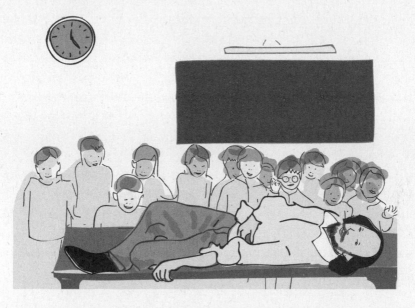

William slowly began to stir and, rubbing his eyes, whispered, "Where am I? Upon what exotic beach have I washed ashore?" The children didn't hesitate for a second, shouting out, "France! You are in Paris!"

Thus the discussion moved to geography. One little boy, Oliver, told Shakespeare that he would soon be moving to another country. He reached to the map of the world on the wall behind him and very accurately showed Shakespeare where France was on the map and where he was going to move — the East Coast of the United States.

Shakespeare asked him if he was going to swim or take a boat to his destination, to which Oliver and many others responded gleefully, "No, a plane!" Oliver then mimed a plane with his outstretched arms.

"Ah, you mean a bird," Shakespeare responded knowingly.

"No, it has no beak," Oliver cried.

"How doth it eat?" asked Shakespeare.

"It doesn't eat!" said Oliver.

"It has a motor, with oil and petrol," explained another boy, Jonah.

"Ah, the mysteries . . ." Shakespeare trailed off.

"That's in our song," Flora joined in.

"You have a song about mysteries?"

The children did, in fact, have a song about mysteries — specifically the mystery surrounding William Shakespeare himself. He said he very much wanted to hear it, so the children launched into the song: "William Shakespeare — Poet and Playwright from Long Long Ago." This was the slightly melancholy theme song of the opera I had written for the occasion.

When they finished, their muse told them that he loved to sing and asked them to teach it to him. Flora began to spontaneously sing *"re re la la sol la fa mi re,"* and the other children joined in. Flora had naturally started to sing "in music," which is what we call singing with note names instead of the French or English lyrics.

Shakespeare smiled. "Ah, that be the music indeed." He listened and carefully repeated the note names and the melody several times, to the delight of the children. Flora then told him that she could play the song on the piano and asked him if he would like her to teach him. He said he would be greatly honored, so this unlikely pair — our six-foot-two Shakespeare in black velvet and gold, and our four-year-old Flora, a study in pink that day, set about teaching and learning the song.

Many of our original songs are carefully written so that the melodies will fit under the five fingers of the children's hands on a piano keyboard. This was the case with the Shakespeare song. Flora said that she had "found" the tune at home on her piano and then added that it was a little like the "Windmill" song. She was spot-on; the Shakespeare song is in the same minor key as the "Windmill" song (described in chapter 2) that the children know well.

The children encouraged Shakespeare as he tentatively sought the notes on the piano. They gently corrected him when he made mistakes, which I suspected he was doing on purpose. When he finally got it right, the children warmly applauded his success. I asked him if I could accompany him, and soon everyone was singing and dancing the Shakespeare song in French, English, and Music.

After we had finished singing the theme song, the Bard invited the children to come into his magical time travel machine with him, and they all jumped on board. He stretched his long white-stockinged legs out on the floor, and the children crowded around him and on him while he made a great ruckus, rocking back and forth and side to side, all the while narrating their travels in song. The children joined in spontaneously singing, dancing, and laughing. They were no longer in twenty-first-century Paris; they were traveling through time with William Shakespeare.

The children's experience with Shakespeare in the classroom was magical — pretend play at its best. Four-year-olds like them gravitate toward magic, music, and the collective creation of a story. They don't experience these elements separately; rather, they intertwine them naturally in their creative and playful little minds.

We have all observed our children pretending to be a mommy or daddy, a doctor, or Peter Pan. Through pretend play, children establish their own laws and bylaws, *and* they enforce them! In pretend play, children are modeling adult behavior, trying it on for size, but *they* are the key actors, not the adults. With musical improvisation, children are also trying to *find* and re-create the music that adults play and listen to. Importantly in both cases, the children are not mimicking or simulating, they are creating! The importance of creative play, and the lack of it in our schools, is coming increasingly to the forefront of public debate. Educators, psychologists, and pediatricians are confirming that without this vital phase in early childhood, we are skipping a critical developmental phase — and the result is decreased autonomy, creativity, and happiness. But at our school, we align ourselves with the research indicating that pretend play is an essential part of early childhood and can influence a child's development.

Of course, creative play does not begin in the fifth year of life. It is a necessary step in the development of theory of mind, which is why we begin it at the youngest possible age. As we saw in chapter 3, two-year-old children learn by modeling themselves after their parents and siblings, and in this way they learn the codes of their family and culture.

By around the time they turn four, however, children are taking this "modeling" to a whole new level: they invent their own stories; they are testing out their understanding of the world and how they fit into the scenario. When given the opportunity, children will use music to crank up the emotional volume of their stories. They will use their understanding of musical universals (low-scary, high-happy) precisely the way film composers do when creating a musical soundtrack. Children can do this with virtually no musical instruction — they learn as they go.

Children participate readily and fearlessly in a group improvisation such as the magical time travel machine that Shakespeare brought to our classroom. They do this not only because it's fun, but also because they need this kind of activity to develop as happy and creative beings. All children will participate, given the opportunity and encouragement.

As we have seen, music is a meta-language that transcends barriers of all kinds. Perhaps when the children attempted to teach Shakespeare their song, they were hoping that in this case, music could transcend a few centuries. They also wanted their song to be a part of the adventure because, as we know well, when a story has a soundtrack, a storm is stormier, and a safe harbor feels safer. Their desire to share their song with Shakespeare also illustrates the social function of music that I have discussed in the preceding chapters.

As children get older and show more intention and initiative, we begin to see more clearly how the science I've been talking about can translate into musical activities, with remarkable benefits. We can delve deeper into musical improvisation and observe young children learning to use musical universals for their own creative needs.

Just as the children in our schools don't have any prior musical training before learning about these universals, you don't need any preprogrammed skills of your own in order to take this journey alongside your child. In fact, children don't even *learn* about basic musical concepts such as major and minor modalities, or about consonance and dissonance, as much as they *feel* the differences between them.

Children are quick to use their new understanding in the creation of their stories, and their caregivers and teachers sometimes have to work to keep up — even though it is up to us to help children take their musical scribbling to another level altogether. But fear not; none of this requires musical training. Your child doesn't have any, and it isn't stopping her!

THE TIGERS AT THE CROSSWALK

We've seen how pretend play and make-believe are part of how children learn the codes of society. Fantasy is especially intoxicating to a four-year-old because of how her brain has developed up to this point in life — and how it hasn't.

A child's brain has fully functional emotional equipment on day one, in the form of her brain's limbic system. Meanwhile, her brain's prefrontal cortex — the seat of executive function, calculation, and judgment — will not fully mature until late adolescence. This temporary triumph of emotion over reason makes the four-year-old brain ideally receptive to wild and exciting stories.

Make-believe play can take place anywhere: at school, in the car, at home, or while walking down the street. You don't need costumes or theater classes; you only need a little whimsy. Ask your child to help you watch out for the tigers while crossing the street! She will share your relief when you safely reach the other side of the road. When you invent a miniature make-believe story like this, you are showing her that amusing stories can be created spontaneously — anywhere, anytime. She will quite naturally assume that she too can invent them. The next day, your four-year-old will take charge and tell you to watch out for the tigers at the crosswalk.

Musical improvisation is another version of make-believe and storytelling. By joining your child in the story and the music she is creating, you are validating her imagination; you are giving her the love and support she needs to believe in her innate creative abilities.

Musical practice in early childhood should ideally resemble pretend play. Children who are encouraged to create their own musical worlds will often spend hours doing so. I must have baffled my parents with my hours spent "playing" the piano, singing, dramatically inventing sagas of danger, courage, love, and redemption. This all occurred long before my first piano lesson. Likewise, three-year-old Émile, whom we met in chapter 3, spent hours at the piano finding and making up songs by the time he turned four. His parents also sent me a film of Émile using a tennis racket as a guitar, singing "Yellow Diamond," a song of his own making, into a microphone that was actually a zucchini. Neither of his parents had any idea where the song came from.

The only thing that Émile's parents or my parents did when they saw this musical experimentation was to encourage it. They didn't have the musical skills to do more. But luckily, at no point did they ever tell us to stop.

In the course of writing this book, I had dinner with an old friend I've known since we were teenaged music students together. I have always admired his skill as a conductor, his incredible ear, his ability to learn music in the blink of an eye, and most of all his absolute passion for music. I asked him about his musical experiences in early childhood. I was interested because his passions include not only classical music but also jazz. Among my friend's award-winning records, there are some jazz recordings. Like many classical musicians, he is not comfortable improvising, so to make the recording, all the improvisations were written down note by note. Given his extraordinary musicality, something didn't add up. I asked him if he had ever sat at the piano as a child and scribbled. His response chilled me: "Yes, I did, but my mother told me to stop."

Émile's and my parents made a musical instrument available to us and left us free to experiment, to scribble. Sometimes this is more than enough. In my case, there was a piano in our basement; I considered it another one of my toys because no one in my family knew how to play it. In Émile's case, I had encouraged his family to buy a piano because Émile was regularly playing the Baby Musicking repertoire on their kitchen table, the sofa, and even the windowsill. My experience has shown me that this initial musical scribbling leads directly to musical improvisation, one of the most complex and compelling of human abilities.

Between the ages of four and five, children have increasingly strong fine motor skills, which they love to try out on any form of keyboard. They seem to instinctively understand that each finger can press on an individual key and produce a sound. Via experimentation, they teach themselves that the sounds become higher as they move to the right and lower as they move to the left. They begin to "pretend play" musically.

We now have thirty years of data surrounding improvisation in early childhood. In my own thirty-five years of experience I can confirm what happens when children are allowed to play with a keyboard: they associate musical sounds with strong emotions and dramatic events. They will create musical storms and elephant stampedes with low notes and soothing lullabies using higher notes.

Children are born with this intuitive understanding of these musical universals, and like Ilyes, whom we met earlier, they make these associations naturally and spontaneously.

Musical improvisation and make-believe play are different expressions of the same creative spark. Most parents enjoy watching their child dress up a younger sibling, giving her precise instructions for dialogue and behavior. Some parents, to their children's delight, will join in the play. This is what I would encourage you to do with your child, even if it takes you a bit outside of your comfort zone!

With your four-year-old, for instance, you can now sit down at a keyboard and begin to invent musical stories. Both of you will go searching for the monsters down in the low notes and the fairies fluttering up in the highest notes. The following exercise requires no previous experience with the piano; rather, it relies on your and your child's understanding of musical universals.

Creating a Musical Soundtrack with Your Child

This exercise can be done with a piano, a xylophone, or a "raid-the-kitchen" collection of larger and smaller pots, pans, and wooden and metal spoons. Don't forget the water jars; you will see that the more water you pour into the glasses, the lower the sound. Try filling at least five glasses so that you can have five different pitches to play with.

For a familiar story to get you started, I've suggested a modified version of "Little Red Riding Hood." Your child will naturally be the main character in her story — so Red is now your daughter (who, for the sake of these examples, I've named Elizabeth). If you have already made a musical name for Elizabeth (see chapter 1), you can use it to begin the story.

• • •

The story begins: *Elizabeth was walking happily through the woods.*

Soundtrack: You both can stroll lightly over the middle and upper parts of the keyboard with one or two fingers, or tap lightly on the smaller pots and pans, while chanting something like "Happy Elizabeth is skipping through the woods." It does not matter which notes you choose, it's more about the light touch, and following the rhythm of the words you are speaking. Gestures are important; don't be afraid to use your entire body. You need to be literally skipping over the keyboard because you are one of the actors in this dramatic story.

The story continues: *Suddenly a nasty wolf appeared.*

Soundtrack: Reach down into the low notes, or larger pans, following the syllables of "big bad wolf" with a short-short-long rhythm. Encourage your child to use all her fingers for this, or to bang loudly.

. . .

Story: *Was Elizabeth afraid? Oh yes, very afraid.*

Soundtrack: Use a horror film technique, utter *dissonance*, meaning using notes that don't sound good together. These are easy to find; they are right next to one another on your keyboard. Show your child how to use one finger on each hand playing a black note and its white note neighbor at the same time, keeping time with the syllables of "Was Elizabeth afraid? Oh yes, very afraid." If you are using jars of water, use your spoons on those that sound the worst together! You and your child can play around with these themes and invent some of your own. These suggestions are only guidelines in case you don't quite know where to start.

Played together, they are very scary

Was Elizabeth afraid?

Story: *Just when Elizabeth was about to be gobbled up by the wolf, her strong and clever grandmother appeared and hit the wolf*

on the head with a frying pan. And the wolf fell down with a tre-
mendous thump!

Soundtrack: A tremendous thump on the lower part of the keyboard is very satisfying, as is an enormous bang on the pots and pans — followed by absolute silence. You will quickly feel the dramatic power of silence and your child will too. We sometimes forget that silence is actually a necessary part of music. Whisper, "Is the wolf dead?" Your child will also begin whispering. There will be no need to ask for this — the story imposes it. Pretend to examine the wolf for signs of life . . . How about the wolf then climbs dizzily to his feet? You can both resume normal voices and slowly begin moving "up" on your various instruments from lower- to higher-pitched sounds. Or maybe the wolf declares that there is a complete misunderstanding, and that he's actually a vegetarian. You can make a celebratory "ta da" moment on your various instruments. Make up any crazy ending you want, or add another chapter to keep the story going.

· · ·

When your child is ready, use nonverbal cues to wind down and end your creation together, holding that last note just a little longer to indicate that your story is over. The more stories you invent, the more comfortable and creative you will become.

Although this exercise does not require that either you or your four-year-old play the piano, it *does* require that you take a risk and begin to explore. If you have no musical training, you and your child will be on equal terms and can experiment together.

What happens if experimentation is never made possible in early childhood, or, worse yet, discouraged? Sometimes the moment passes; the flame dies out, as it did with my conductor friend. I have many friends who are extraordinary classically trained musicians, who still somehow feel very uncomfortable without a score in front of them.

You can avoid this outcome by simply giving your child the opportunity to experiment — and not stopping her when she does so. If a child has access to a musical instrument, not only will they begin experimenting and creating musical stories, but also they will teach themselves to play the songs that they love. It is quite astonishing; they begin to re-create the music of their household and their culture via trial and error — learning to "speak" in music just as they are learning to speak their native language(s). But with their newfound motor skills, children in their fifth year are able to "speak" using musical instruments. They will speak/play to their heart's content — and possibly make your neighbors wish you had never purchased that musical instrument.

FINDING "THAT" SONG

Most children, when trying to reproduce a familiar melody, keep at it until they have found the song they want to hear. Many will stick with it until they know their song from beginning to end. It might take a little time for some children to get their heads around notes that aren't consecutive on the scale (Do, Re, Mi, etc). Those non-consecutive notes may also be tricky for little fingers to navigate, but the children all find the path sooner or later. Then they memorize the map. They have not been taught a piece of music; instead, they are discovering how to find the music they want to hear, all on their own.

We've watched this happen so many times, when children find themselves at a keyboard. Generally this entails a simple tune such as "Happy Birthday," or in France "Frère Jacques." The children start on one note, perhaps Do. If the song is "Frère Jacques," they find that moving "up," playing Do-Re-Mi, gives them the first three notes. Then they struggle because the next necessary note is Do, which means going back down, skipping over one note on the way. We see them struggle with these nonconsecutive notes, but then persist until they finally find the pattern. This is not music theory, this is musicking. This is not rote memorization, this is creative problem solving.

Finding a melody on a piano or a xylophone is very different from being taught a piece of music by reading a score. The latter involves reading and execution. But finding or inventing a song is teaching oneself about melody, rhythm, and harmony through creative experimentation. Children learn language in precisely this manner. They manipulate nouns and verbs, but very few four-year-olds can understand the rules of grammar or the parts of speech.

Learning anything by rote is top-down and inappropriate for this age group, as I have mentioned. Learning through creative experimentation, moreover, will be robust and durable. Most importantly, when the motivation and initiation are internal rather than imposed from the outside, it can support self-esteem and lead to greater experimentation. Imagine that by merely providing a keyboard for your four-year-old and inviting her to find a song, you are giving her a giant, delicious dose of autonomy and creative problem-solving skills.

As we have seen in the preceding chapters, children are musically enculturated by their first birthday. At the age of four, they are already experts in the musical syntax of their culture. For example, when children improvise with their teachers, the teacher will lead the child toward the end of the improvisation. At that point the child instinctively wanders back to the first note of the scale of the piece, because this is a harmonic rule in all Western music. Children have an unconscious or implicit understanding of this rule. They don't need to be told to "resolve to the tonic," which is the musical terminology. They just do it because if feels right. We call it "going home."

WHO'S AFRAID OF IMPROVISATION?

We've been talking a lot about improvisation, but where does it come from, and what is its true nature? Improvisation simply means to play music or speak or otherwise act or perform without prior preparation. Improvisation is unplanned and spontaneous, and is a constant part of our lives, from coming up with a new excuse for being late to work to throwing together some ingredients in the kitchen. Mozart and Beethoven actually improvised all the time in their public performances. One common practice in their day was to improvise a set of variations based on a popular tune suggested by an audience member. When they performed their own concertos, these composers would improvise the cadenza, the part at the end of each movement when the orchestra rests and the featured soloist plays alone.

There was a fine line between improvisation and composition at the time. In purely practical terms, there was simply less written music available, and sometimes a composer would write down a particularly satisfying improvisation as part of a piece of music. I often tell children that if Johann Sebastian Bach needed a piece of music for his son's birthday party, he had to write it himself.

By the beginning of the twentieth century, improvisation had all but disappeared from classical music. Some scholars believe that by this time, there was simply too much music to learn, so classical performers spent their time memorizing existing scores and slowly stopped creating music themselves. Improvisation used to be taught in all music schools, but this ended in the early twentieth century. The last known classical improvisation class was at the Hochschule für Musik und Kunst in Berlin in 1904.

The "raid-the-kitchen" question-and-answer game from chapter 3 is not only a wacky dialogue with pots and pans but also an improv exercise. You don't even have to have a musical instrument to improvise. We all possess the most versatile musical instruments in the world: our bodies and our voices. We can put words to a melody and accompany ourselves by clapping and stomping.

So far, if you've been doing the exercises that accompany the text, you've invented a rhythmic question-and-answer game, a musical name for your child, and a personal nursery rhyme. Now, in the next exercise, you are ready to make up an entire song. Your four-year-old will be thrilled, she will probably help you, and she will always remember "her song."

Creating a Song with Your Child: Structure and Improvisation

For this exercise, we will create a basic, repetitive piece of music, with one opening for improvisation. That section can change each time the song is sung. If you are not comfortable inventing a new melody, take an old one like "Mary Had a Little Lamb" and fit your words to it.

Remember that one of the essential elements of simple songs is the refrain, or chorus. The younger the child, the more she needs the predictability of repetition. In this song exercise (we'll use the melody of "Mary Had a Little Lamb"), the first line is repeated twice, and only the last line changes. This is where the improvisation comes in. You and your child can take turns inventing the last line and let anyone else join in the fun.

It might sound something like this:

My delightful Isabella
Isabella, Isabella
My delightful Isabella
Improv: Loves her teddy bear
    . . . loves her leafy greens
    . . . loves her baby brother
    . . . wants to learn to fly
    . . . loves to make up songs

We have already noted how strong the emotional factor is in music, so you can see how this could quickly become her favorite song. That you are creating this for her and with her is powerful, very different from pushing the play button on a device.

The next step in our improv adventure is a hands-on moment — literally. We will be combining many of the traits and abilities that we've seen children develop so far, from their motor skills to their love of pretend play, and applying them toward something new: the translation of music from their heads to an instrument, in a way that will give them tools to keep experimenting. The instrument in this case will be the piano. But even if you have never touched a piano before, remember that all of these musicking games were created for very young children — so there's absolutely nothing you can't handle!

OUR MUSICAL HAND

Imagine a bright and colorful music room with three pianos, two xylophones, two congas, and a drum kit. One of the upright pianos is entirely open, so that children can watch the ballet of hammers on the strings inside the piano when it is played. The children love this spectacle. In fact, they love everything about this music room. Each campus has a dedicated music room filled with naked pianos, drums, and xylophones.

Now picture our four-year-olds, Hector, Alex, Lizzy, and Constance, dancing their way into the room where Aurélien, their teacher, is waiting for them. He welcomes them and explains that since they are now four years old, which is very big, they will be learning to play the piano just like the older children.

Aurélien sits down on the floor, leans over, and whispers to the children, "I have a secret to tell you." The children are immediately captivated, and he whispers even more quietly, "There is a musical note living inside each of your fingers."

The children are skeptical. They look at their fingers, and impudent Hector holds his index finger to his ear and says, *"Je n'entends rien"*— "I don't hear anything."

Aurélien laughs. "You don't believe me?" He starts tapping his thumb on the floor to the Do-domino rhythm, while sonorously singing the little motif on pitch. He then goes to the piano and plays the motif on a Do. The fact that it is the same sound makes it really seem like the Do does live in Aurélien's thumb. The children begin singing Do-domino, of course, and tapping their thumbs on the floor.

The children are used to dancing the scale, but this is the first time they are associating the musical scale with their hands. Aurélien then shows them his index finger and asks them, "Who do you think lives here?" Alex sings out, "Re–a rainbow!" When Aurélien shows his third finger, the children are already on to him; all four of them shout out, "Mi-mmeow! Then their teacher pretends to be very frightened while showing them his fourth finger. He uses his best ghostly voice, and with a look of terror sings, "Fa-phantom!" The children love it, and soon everyone is pretending that their fourth fingers are demonic. Sunny Sol is last, but not least.

After the children have learned which of their fingers contains which musical note, their teacher begins singing Do-Re-Mi-Fa-Sol up and down, while the children fold and unfold their fingers — the thumb for Do, the index finger for Re, and so on — until they can easily move each finger to correspond to each note .

Then suddenly, Aurélien unexpectedly sings Do-Sol-Do. After a moment of surprise, the children fold their thumbs and fifth fingers while singing Do-Sol-Do. There we are: they have understood the idea of their "musical hand."

Then the class moves to the piano. The children have already learned to find a Do on the keyboard by locating the group of two black notes.

Their teacher invites each one of them to the piano to play the Do-domino with their thumbs. Lizzy can't restrain herself from continuing to play Re–a rainbow with her index finger. Constance, not to be outdone, sings and plays Mi-meow with her third finger. And so the children continue testing their newfound musical skills by translating what is in their fingers to the keys.

Over the coming weeks, the four-year-olds go from being able to find the melodies that Aurélien sings to them with note names, to finding the melodies he hums without the note names. This is the piano-based version of musical hide-and-seek with musical pitches that we saw in the previous chapter. They also play another game —

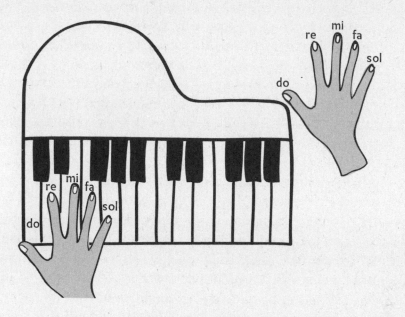

one of their favorites — that involves their teacher miming a melody with his fingers that he is sure they will recognize. The children love it when they tentatively begin to sing what their teacher is miming, and then suddenly, one of them recognizes the song: 1-1-5-5 or Re Re–La La: "Oh, it's William Shakespeare!" someone will exclaim.

When this game becomes fluid, the children go to the piano and start the game over again, this time with the teacher humming the beginning of a song that they can hardly wait to play. The children feel both joy and accomplishment when a song that they know well comes to life under their own fingers.

The ability to swiftly find a melody on a keyboard gives way to the invention of their own melodies. We have always encouraged them to invent their own music, reminding them that when J. S. Bach was alive, he *had* to write new music because there simply wasn't enough available! They use their new compositions to play the note name guessing games with their teachers and peers, and they are, of course, always trying to win by stumping their friends. The sound and feel of the musical pitches are reinforced with a new physical reference, the child's hand. When the child can sing a melody while miming it with his hand, moving to the keyboard is the natural next step. Imagine the excitement when they realize that they can already hear which note is under each finger.

This kind of bottom-up learning leads to an organic relationship between pitch and the children's hands. We can verify this by humming a melody that stays within the notes under the child's hand, only to hear them play it back to us, often singing the note names as well.

Many classically trained pianists cannot do what these four-year-olds can, even if they can rip through a Tchaikovsky concerto, because they weren't exposed to aural transmission and embodiment learning. Our four-year-olds can hear a simple melody, translate it directly to their hands, and then to a musical instrument, because they hear the notes that lie under each finger in their heads. If you hear and feel a song in your body and mind, producing it on a musical instrument is almost automatic. With the following exercise, you will understand how melodies or songs move up and down or left to right, and how quickly your hands can master this.

Hide-and-Seek with Your Musical Hand

Now that you have mastered the musical note name game with your body, it's time to transfer your nascent skills to your hand.

First, sit down next to your child so that your hands are not mirroring. Keep your xylophone or another pitched instrument nearby for accuracy.

Now, like our students' theatrical music teacher Aurélien, tell your child that a Do-domino lives in the thumb of your right hand. Tap your thumb on the floor, make it dance to the jazzy Do-domino (having secretly checked your pitch with your xylophone). Ask her to tap her thumb on the floor as well, and you can sing together.

Then bring out the xylophone and verify that it is the same pitch. Do-domino really does live in your child's thumb. Repeat with your fifth finger, making the little finger fly high in the sky before gently descending to the floor to play Sol-sunshine.

Before moving on to the remaining three notes, play the game of folding your fingers while singing Sol-Do or Do-Sol and Do-Sol-Do. Then comes the dreadful Fa-phantom — children love this one!

Move on slowly over a period of weeks until you and your child are comfortable with all five notes and can play miming games with all five. Then, if you have a piano, you can begin to play with your musical hands on the keyboard. There is no end to the variations that you can try.

The more you play this game, the more your child will develop her sensitivity to musical pitches and how this relates to her body and to a musical instrument. This exercise can also be the beginning of "finding a song." You can mime the beginning of a song your child knows while singing the pitches. Then try it without singing the pitches, and see how quickly she grasps the concept.

This ability is widespread in non-Western musical cultures; one has to learn to "play by ear" because there are no scores on which to rely. We achieve the same effect in our classrooms by choice rather than necessity.

When children begin their musical journey by learning to read musical notation, they will forever be reliant on the written score. By contrast, playing by ear, or having a "good ear," is not about being musically "gifted" or having years of conservatory training; it simply is the way that our forefathers practiced music. Don't be worried that your child will never learn to read music if she has learned to play by ear. There is no relationship between the two. A good music teacher will guide your child through this process — which for many children is a wonderful "breaking the code" moment. If this is not the case, change teachers!

Perhaps best of all, this style of playing allows us to spontaneously join in all forms of music making. We can join the band because we have established a natural sensory link to the music. In learning music this way, moreover, we are not actually breaking from the grand tradition of Western musical training; rather, we are following in it.

GUIDO D'AREZZO AND *HIS* MUSICAL HAND

The Western music system actually has its roots in the musical hand of a medieval Benedictine monk. Guido d'Arezzo, who lived circa AD 990–1050, was born in Arezzo, a small Italian town in what is now the region of Tuscany. At the time, there was no musical notation. To learn a new piece of music, you had to listen to a performance, or someone who had memorized the piece needed to teach you by rote. It seems safe to assume that Guido was a frustrated young monk, finding it dreadfully tedious to teach new melodies to singers note by note. He may also have feared that music in his monastery was being unreliably transmitted, and suspected darkly that certain compositions were being deliberately altered by some of the ambitious young monks in training.

If necessity is the mother of invention, we can assume that, in his frustration, Guido felt compelled to create some way to make a permanent record of these songs — a musical notation system. This is the equivalent of singlehandedly inventing an alphabet, which, in the case of the Roman alphabet, was a collective effort involving several emerging civilizations and evolving over thousands of years. How did Guido do it alone?

He began by giving a name to the seven musical pitches that made up the scale already widely in use at the time. (The seven-note scale is present in almost all music.) He chose the first syllables of the words of a Latin hymn as a base, attributing a syllable to each note of the scale:

Ut queant laxis [Ut later became Do]
Resonare fibris
Mira gestorum
Famuli tuorum
Solve polluti
Labii reatum,
Sancte Iohannes

(*Ti* was invented by Rodgers and Hammerstein for the song "Do-Re-Mi" in the Broadway musical *The Sound of Music*. It was never used in music theory or practice. The correct original syllable is *Si*, pronounced like "see.")

Guido then developed a stave with four lines, a sort of graphic ladder on which notes climb up and down. In AD 1200 a fifth line was added, and this five-line system of musical notation remains unchanged today.

I still marvel at musical notation. When one looks at a full sym-

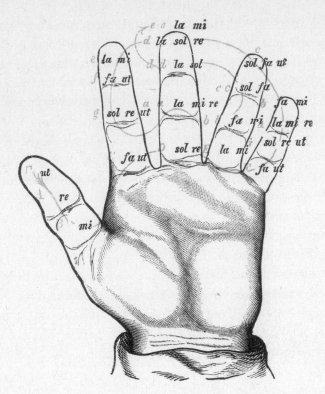

phonic score, it is almost impossible to imagine that those lines and dots carry within them the magic of a beautiful work.

Guido d'Arezzo is also famous for "Guido's hand," an elaborate system for learning and memorizing music using each part of the human hand as a reference point for a musical pitch. Guido's musical hand uses every part of the hand, beginning with the base of the thumb, then moving up and down the fingers — joints and all — spanning a total of three octaves. The creation of this musical hand allowed him to teach music to singers before musical notation actually existed.

Guido had created what we now call a mnemonic device, a code that reinforces memory. Mnemonic devices are especially useful when they involve the human body. Our young charges in the classroom are following in his footsteps. Or should I say, handprints?

Western musical notation is very accessible to young children, if they can approach it with their bodies and voices. We are not teaching them to read music at the age of four, but we are showing them how a melody is related to space vertically, and rhythm to space horizontally. When a melody moves up, the symbols (notes) move vertically up the staff. A whole note (four beats) takes up more space horizontally than a quarter note (one beat). The notions of up and down in music need to be experienced with the child's body. Otherwise they remain an abstraction. By having the children move up and down while singing, then associating musical pitches with their fingers, this abstraction becomes a physical reality.

This fun-filled training in early childhood establishes implicit musical knowledge and pitch memory. This organic musical experience in early childhood helps young people develop a visceral relationship to music — enabling them to look at a musical score later in life and hear it in their mind, and to hear a piece of music with no score and spontaneously join in the jam. Teaching children to read music before they have experienced melody and rhythm in their bodies will disrupt their natural musical development.

MUSICAL CONSTRUCTIONS

One morning, four-year-old Margot was participating in a musical piece that had no written score. The children were learning what I call a *musical construction*. This is a child-size version of what Bobby McFerrin does with "circle songs" and Ben Folds does with orchestras. In their musical constructions, each group of people or instruments is given a specific musical motif that they will continue to repeat, while other groups join in one by one, thus creating a glorious musical layer cake.

The children were to present this particular musical construction, which we called "The Music We Share," at an educational conference later in the month. It consisted of short melodic and rhythmic fragments, some to be sung and others to be played on various instruments, that would layer upon one another. The children were also invited to improvise solos. Once all of the layers had been added, we would invite the audience to sing "Frère Jacques" on top, and it would all fit together harmoniously. The children loved practicing this together, and requested it all the time. Margot was one of the singers, and her musical motif was *mi mi mi mi mi sol mi re do mi re do.*

After we practiced the piece, Margot went off to the reading and writing part of the preschool morning. As it was nearing lunchtime, Margot's French teacher came to see me. She asked if I could come into the classroom for a moment.

When I got to the classroom, Margot was there, and she proudly showed me a small board with magnetic letters. It took me a moment to understand what I was seeing. Margot, who was learning to read, had "written" her melody in magnetic letters — *mi mi mi mi mi sol mi re do mi re do* — entirely on her own.

Margot told me that she had made this because she loved what she called "my music" and wanted to teach it to her little sister. The fact that Margot's two-year-old sister could not read was apparently of no importance. What mattered was that Margot had created her

own little mnemonic device to help her remember the melody she wanted to share with her sister. Of course, as an educator I was thrilled to see Margot putting together her musical learning with her emerging understanding of reading and writing.

As we saw in the previous chapter, we don't need to learn to read music to make music. But as Guido discovered, without it, our ability to learn is constrained by our ability to memorize. Musical notation allows us to learn more and more pieces. The same holds true for reading and writing. With the arrival of a written form of language, news could be shared, history recorded, love letters written.

Guido d'Arezzo, we've theorized, created his particular spatial system to spare us the boredom of obligatory memorization. Little could he have known that centuries later, his system would be used to torture music students in some parts of the world, owing to the gradual loss of a critical developmental step: we need to learn language and music first orally before we can understand their written form.

As I have pointed out, children learn to read once they already know how to speak. Reading is a matter of understanding the graphic representations of something they've already mastered, their native language. But unfortunately, many children's musical educations do not follow this same intuitive pathway. In the Western classical music tradition, music education begins with instrumental lessons around the age of seven, and it starts with learning to read music, which is to say that children are very often asked to read music before they "speak" it, before they've had the experience of making music.

We would never try to teach a child to read the printed word before they could use words to communicate. So why do we do this for music? This unnatural process discourages many children long before they experience the pleasure of playing with a musical instrument. Victor Wooten, the Grammy Award–winning bassist who learned to play music by trying to keep up with his siblings, puts it quite succinctly: "The end of the child's musical life just might be the day of his first music lesson."

MOODS AND MODES

We should keep in mind that many people teach themselves to play musical instruments. I have met many a self-taught musician, and although they might experience some technical difficulties down the road, they generally have a very spontaneous and emotional relationship to the moods and modes of music.

A musical mode is simply a seven-note scale. These scales, along with the interval of a perfect fifth, were given their descriptive names in ancient Greece. This is not surprising, because as we saw in chapter 3, music is not arbitrary; it involves vibrations that obey physical laws. Pythagoras had already figured this out in the fifth century BC. He postulated that everything in the world was related to mathematics — including music. Rumor has it that he was the first person to cut a string in half and note that the sound it made was exactly the same sound produced by the full-length string, just higher — exactly one octave (eight notes) higher. He also discovered that when a string vibrates, it actually contains a series of "overtones," or secondary vibrations that come about in a natural and fixed order.

As Pythagoras observed, the first note in the overtone series is the *same* note one octave higher, so first low Do, then high Do. The next vibration in the series is a Sol, five notes higher than Do. The interval or distance between Do and Sol is called a perfect fifth. Pythagoras probably called it "perfect" because the vibrations of the two notes are so similar that they almost sound like one note — no dreaded dissonance between the two. The perfect fifth serves as an anchor or primal building block in almost all of the world's musical constructions.

There is a phenomenon linked to our five fingers that I find magical. When a child puts her right hand on the white keys of the piano, beginning with a thumb on Do, her fifth finger falls on Sol. When she plays these two notes together, she is playing a "perfect fifth." If she moves over by one note and plays a Re with her thumb, her fifth finger will be on La; once again, they create a perfect fifth.

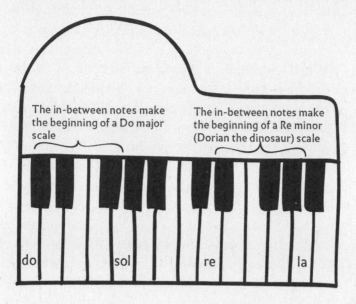

The in-between notes make the beginning of a Do major scale

The in-between notes make the beginning of a Re minor (Dorian the dinosaur) scale

do   sol   re   la

The perfect fifth is at the center of virtually every musical system in the world today — even music that we imagine shares nothing with our Western tradition. The *tanpura,* the instrument that provides the constant "drone" sound underlying Indian classical music, creates a perfect fifth; the four strings of a violin are separated by a fifth; our system of scales is based on a "circle of fifths," and the chords that stem from the perfect fifth (with one added middle note) are the basis of all harmony in the Western world.

The perfect fifth created by Do and Sol is the skeleton of both a Do major and a Do minor chord, but if the child plays all the white keys in between Do and Sol, we have the beginning of the Do major scale. When you place your thumb on the note next to Do, a Re, your fifth finger will fall on La. This again is a perfect fifth, and will sound equally harmonious. This is because the frequencies of the two notes that make up a perfect fifth are very similar: they go together so well that you might wonder if you are even hearing two different notes.

Although it is a complete coincidence that the human hand naturally falls on the modern keyboard as a perfect fifth, I usually manage to convince the younger children that this is magic, proof that we were born to play the piano. The perfect fifth sounds almost neutral all by itself. You can move around the keyboard playing different notes but keeping your thumb and pinky finger a five-note distance apart. You won't hear much of a difference. But when you play all of the notes *between* those two anchor notes (the beginning of a scale), each one will "feel" very different. Pythagoras gave each one of the modes or scales a name that he thought described their character. If you start on a Do and move up the keyboard to the next Do, you have the Ionian or major scale. The following modes, Re to Re, Mi to Mi, and so on, are Dorian, Phrygian, Lydian, Mixolydian, Aeolian, and Locrian.

Two of my favorite classroom memories involve modes and the spontaneous attribution of emotional valence by very young children. The children have by now become very adept at knowing the notes that "live in their fingers," so we can spice things up and leave the "first position." Four-year-old Sam's teacher asked him to come to the piano and place his right hand on Re. This means that the notes under his five fingers were the beginning of a scale in the Dorian minor mode. Sam improvised for a few minutes with his teacher gently accompanying him. When he finished, he said that this was "dinosaur music." "What do you mean, Sam?" his teacher asked. "Dinosaurs don't exist, which is sad, and this music is sad." Ever since, the Dorian scale is referred to as Dorian the Dinosaur in our classrooms.

On another day I was having children improvise with their right thumb on a Mi. This means they have their fingers on Mi, Fa, Sol, La, Si, which is called the Phrygian mode, and is not commonly used. It sounds very dissonant, and even contains a tritone interval, once considered the "devil's interval." An interval is the space between two notes: unison, second, third, and so on. There are intervals that Westerners hear as harmonious (the major and minor thirds, the perfect fifth) and some dissonant intervals (the minor second and the devilish tritone). This is a function of the compatibility of acoustic frequencies. Just as lower pitches sound somber

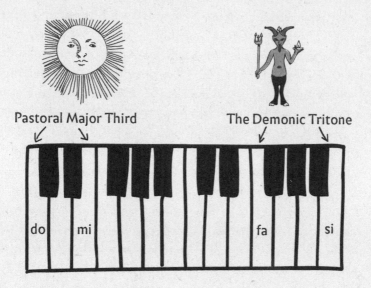

Pastoral Major Third   The Demonic Tritone

or scary in almost all musical cultures, humans find dissonant intervals jarring.

In the case of the tritone between Fa and Si in a Do major scale, it hits the ear like the proverbial fingernails on a blackboard because of the incompatibility of the two notes' frequencies. It is not surprising that this interval is rarely found in melodies anywhere in the world—making it paradoxically a musical universal! In the Phrygian mode, the first and second notes of the scale are separated by a half step, not the whole step that we are accustomed to. The result is that we never feel as though we are "going home," that is, bringing the song full circle and finishing on the note we started with, or "resolving to the tonic."

Rambunctious four-year-old Maya was laughing out loud one day while improvising with me in the Phrygian mode; we were both getting a bit raucous. I asked her what she thought about the music we were making together, and she said, "It sounds like music from another planet." We decided to name our piece "Freaky Phrygian."

Learning to Play, Playing to Learn

I've seen the most musically inexperienced parents learn to improvise with their children. Just sit down at a piano or any kind of keyboard and play Do and Sol (perfect fifth) simultaneously, or one after the other, with a rhythm that you enjoy. An easy one is *short-short-long* or "big bad wolf . . . big bad wolf . . ." You may notice that this is the *stomp-stomp-clap* rhythm that Brian May, the lead guitarist from the group Queen, used to ask audience members to perform while the group played their iconic "We Will Rock You." May believed this simple rhythm would provide a throbbing backbeat to this rousing anthem, and be a fun and easy way for the audience to join in the music making. He was right; this rhythm can bring an entire stadium of people into synchronization because of its primal structure — the proportion of two to one.

Baby can play anything on the white keys

Begin your own perfect fifth ostinato (repeating motif) and invite your child to play any of the white notes of the keyboard along with you. It is not important how or what she plays at first. She may be using both hands or just one finger; it doesn't matter. You will see that your child begins to play in sync with you. You will also notice that you and your child will come "home" to the tonic (Do) when you are ready to wind down and end your improvisation. When you're playing comfortably in sync, you can decide together how you would like to play. You might ask your child what animal she would like to incarnate or what story she would like to tell.

Now move your thumb and fifth finger up one note to the Re and La. You will feel the difference and so will your child. This is the minor scale that our Sam named "Dorian the Dinosaur." If you are feeling wildly confident, you can move between the two positions. Another option is the "Zebra." Ask your child if she sees anything black and white on the piano that reminds her of a zebra. The "Zebra" game entails jumping from the black notes to the white notes at regular intervals. For this, you will need to move your hand from Do-Sol to Do#-Sol# (in musical notation, a # is a "sharp"). On a keyboard, these are the black keys that are found to the right of Do and Sol.

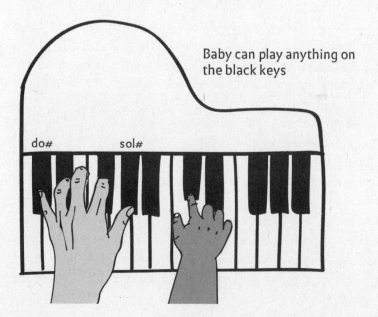

Baby can play anything on the black keys

do#   sol#

The interval is still a perfect fifth, and it will feel exactly the same under your hand. Now ask your child to play only the black notes. You will both instantly hear that you have entered into a new harmonic world. The black notes of a piano make up the exotic pentatonic (five-note) scale that we will look at in the next chapter. You are making music with your child, exploring harmony and synchronization together, a moment of shared creation that far surpasses any other musical experience you might consider purchasing.

THE CREATIVITY QUEST

These stories and exercises show us how much can be learned about music simply through creative exploration. I have seen how fast children learn and how much they love to learn through experimentation and even pretend play with music. Music is the subject of this book, but the larger question of creative exploration and pretend play in early childhood has been abundantly studied. One of the first to observe the benefits of pretend play was the Russian developmental psychologist Lev Vygotsky. Vygotsky's theories are now almost a century old, but these insights continue to shed light on the role of play in child development in general and the development of self-regulation in particular. We already have longitudinal studies on the subject of creativity — spanning more than fifty years and counting. And yet . . .

There remains a divide in many developed countries concerning the merits of structured learning versus imagination and free play in all areas, from the arts and humanities to science and math. We can see the extent of the gap just by observing when education becomes mandatory in different countries around the world. In Germany and Finland, school begins at six and seven years of age, respectively. In France, school starts at three, ever since the government created *l'école maternelle* in the late nineteenth century to keep children off the streets.

What goes on in preschools and kindergartens around the globe ranges from "Outward Bound"–style programs in which kids roam the woods in Germany; to free play and life skills learning in Finland; to reading, writing, math, English, and, finally, daily homework in Shanghai. New recipes for brain boosts become fads very quickly because parents everywhere are determined to provide children with any available advantage. In highly developed economies this cognitive race is getting out of hand. Nobody ever went broke exploiting parental anxiety, even though so many of the apps and gadgets and programs on offer are essentially useless. As we saw with the "Mozart effect," some ideas become wildly popular and yet have absolutely no scientific basis. Most of the promised effects of recent very early reading programs and Baby Genius products are not panning out in longitudinal studies.

In the midst of this, we have a plethora of meaningful and useful information that isn't reaching parents and educators fast enough. The work of the experts I have discussed — Malloch, Trevarthen, Bruner, Patel, Koelsch, and Kuhl — all give clear scientific indications of how the brain works, of when and how children learn or don't learn. The irony is that if we listened to what the carefully researched, study-backed hard science is telling us, we would not need to purchase a thing. We would be content to allow our children to grow and develop through loving, playful, and musical exchanges with us, our families, and our communities.

Future-oriented thinkers are looking long and hard at what the twenty-first-century child will need to know to thrive in a vastly changing world. The idea of imaginative play is gaining traction, and educators are beginning to accept that the high-tech skills race isn't enough, and that imagination, confidence, social skills, and happiness, will be — as they always have been — keys to success in life. The American Academy of Pediatrics (AAP) is calling our attention to the dangers of the current IQ sweepstakes. "The importance of playful learning for children cannot be overemphasized," indicates the academy's 2018 clinical report "The Power of Play." "The lifelong success of children is based on their ability to be creative and to apply the lessons learned from playing." Music, art, and creative playtime have all but disappeared from our children's schools in the past fifty years. The amount of play, improvisation, and creative thinking has never been so low, nor reports of depression and anxiety as high, according to the AAP.

The highest-rated school system in the world, according to the Organization for Economic Cooperation and Development (OECD), the World Economic Forum, and UNICEF, is in Finland. In this school system, the happiness of children is the first priority. The children enjoy play breaks every hour, and play is considered the most essential element of the children's physical, mental, and social development.

Music is an intrinsic part of the Finnish educational curriculum; in fact, it is mandatory from first through sixth grades. Before that, music making is organized in day care centers, where the focus is on play and creativity. Certification for day care employees and primary school teachers includes training in music and musicking. In Finland, there are eighty-nine government-subsidized specialized music schools, as well as forty-one other schools that teach dance, visual arts, and crafts. These schools work hand in hand with the comprehensive school system and provide what is called the "basic education in the arts." Interestingly, in specialized music schools, 36 percent of the enrollment is made up of preschoolers!

The prominent role of music in the Finish model is rarely mentioned when the success of the educational system is discussed. I find this a very strange oversight. I see two possible explanations. The first is that we are still stubbornly unwilling to recognize the importance of music in our children's development. The second explanation is fear: our chronic Western world fear of musical inadequacy. We can't seem to believe that musical expertise is not required for us to make music together, either as children or as adults. When we speak of making music, we say that we are *playing* music, and yet we have become terribly afraid of doing just that: playing.

Throughout this chapter, we have had several opportunities to appreciate the spontaneous, creative musicking ability of four-year-olds. Innovative learning and experimentation come about because children are *attracted* to music and will try to produce it themselves spontaneously when given the opportunity. When children in the classroom want to show me what they have "found" on the piano, or when parents share the videos they make of their children inventing music at home, I see young people who are demonstrating focus, flexibility, self-motivation, and creative perseverance — traits that will likely serve them far better in real life than IQ points alone, never mind rote memorization of musical scores.

The so-called "father of creativity" is the psychologist E. Paul Torrance. He began his career as a teacher, an experience that made him acutely aware of the lack of training or information available to teachers who were faced with children who did not respond well to traditional classroom teaching. In an attempt to solve this problem, he inadvertently started a revolution in the study of creativity — and helped show how important this trait in particular is to children's success and satisfaction in life.

In the 1940s, Torrance began researching creativity as a means of helping teachers and improving American education. His insight was that to understand and encourage creativity, we first needed to define it, then measure and analyze it. Torrance had a hunch that IQ was not the only meaningful metric for determining human potential, and that perhaps the American education system had involuntarily created programs that furthered social injustice instead of reducing it.

Torrance was one of the first psychologists to posit that artistic creativity and the creativity shown by scientists, teachers, or business entrepreneurs might be one and the same. He was convinced that traditional IQ tests did not take into consideration the ability to think creatively about new situations or problems. His test, which he revised five different times over a forty-year period, is still in use today. Some of my favorite questions on the test include:

- Just Suppose: An unusual situation is described, and the subject is asked to predict the possible outcomes when a new element or variable is introduced.
- Improvement Task: The subject is given a list of everyday objects and is asked to suggest as many ways as they can to improve each object. The possible improvements do not have to be based on reality.
- The Cow Jumped Over the Moon: The task is to think of all possible things that might happen when a cow jumps over the moon.

After the subjects of Torrance's test have given their answers to these questions, the responses are then evaluated with the following criteria:

- Fluency: the total number of interpretable, meaningful, and relevant ideas generated in response to the stimulus
- Flexibility: the number of different categories of relevant responses
- Originality: the unusualness of the responses
- Elaboration: the amount of detail in the responses

To date, several longitudinal studies have been conducted to follow up the elementary school–aged students who were first administered the Torrance Tests of Creative Thinking in 1958. There has been a twenty-two-year follow-up, a forty-year follow-up, and a fifty-year follow-up. The follow-up studies have continued to evolve to take into consideration such dramatic variables as the Vietnam War and severe personal hardship.

These studies continue to find that students identified as creatively gifted but not intellectually gifted consistently achieve more than the intellectually gifted in adulthood. These achievements range from patented inventions to designing clothes, computer programs, and business models or building a home. The question of pure personal satisfaction was also asked of the participants. Torrance was already interested in how people rated their own happiness — long before the idea of "Gross National Happiness" became a phenomenon.

Another of Torrance's findings was that creative thinking abilities differ from the abilities involved in intelligence and logical reasoning. In fact, the use of IQ tests to identify gifted students can miss up to 70 percent of those who score the highest in tests such as the Torrance Tests. In a study from 2011, Torrance's data were analyzed yet again. The research team involved found that the correlation to lifetime creative accomplishment was more than three times stronger for childhood creativity than for childhood IQ.

What I find so moving about Torrance's work is that it didn't concern itself with "thinking outside the box" or "finding the flow" or any of the other simple catchphrases that consume people today. Torrance wasn't looking to unleash the next Thomas Edison or Henry Ford, and he'd never heard of Bill Gates or Steve Jobs. Torrance simply was concerned that we might be misjudging some of our finest minds and condemning bright, creative children to failure just because schools chose to evaluate only IQ.

This remains a problem today. The OECD, via its Program for International Student Assessment (PISA), confirms that schools the world over continue to focus on content memorization rather than creative problem solving. An alarming study was conducted in 2010 by Kyung Hee Kim at the College of William & Mary in Virginia. Kim analyzed almost 300,000 Torrance scores of children and adults and found that creativity scores had steadily risen, just like IQ scores, until 1990. Since then, creativity scores have been decreasing. Sadly, in her study it was the scores of the youngest children that showed the steepest decline.

Paul Torrance summed up his conclusions neatly and simply: "People prefer to learn creatively — by exploring, questioning, experimenting, manipulating, re-arranging things, testing and modifying, listening, looking, feeling — and then thinking about it — incubating." No one who has spent time in one of the classrooms at L'École Koenig can have any doubt about this statement. Think of what our four-year-olds are doing when they sit at a piano and look for a melody: they are *exploring* and *experimenting*. When they try different note combinations and rhythms, they are *manipulating, rearranging things, testing and modifying, listening, looking*. They are *feeling* and attributing emotional valence to their impressions. When Margot reproduced the syllables of her song on her magnetic board all on her own, she was thinking about it — what Torrance calls *incubating*. She had effortlessly connected so many dots that her teachers were speechless. Little did Margot know that she had just produced an extraordinary example of creative problem solving and transversal thinking.

The stories from this chapter demonstrate how, between the ages of four and five, children need fantasy and pretend play. Children want to invent stories, songs, and dances in which they are the stars and we the adults are supporting actors at best. This is the child's way of testing the world in which she lives and her own place in it.

When I see young children engaged in musical improvisation, I know that there is something profound taking place; this is not just about the child choosing notes and rhythms. The music cognition specialist Richard Ashley elegantly addresses these deeper implications: "Improvisation is not an isolated side issue with regard to human music-making; it connects musical structure, our bodies, and our sense of ourselves as individuals and as members of social units in powerful ways."

When children are allowed to improvise and create music together, a spark is ignited, and the fireworks begin. At the age of four, this is a crucial part of the development of their creativity and confidence. We don't want to let that moment pass just because we feel silly, or because we are insecure about our own natural musicality. We certainly don't want to let that moment pass because we have bought into the cognitive rat race, mistakenly thinking that IQ is everything. It isn't.

TAKING WING

As she approaches her fifth birthday, your child is a sentient cognitive sponge. She absorbs knowledge and new experiences at a staggering rate and is increasingly autonomous. The philosopher Immanuel Kant defined the "Age of Enlightenment" as the age at which one begins to dare think for oneself. Kant borrowed this idea, *"Sapere Aude"* (Latin for "dare to know"), from the Roman poet Horace (65–8 BC) — making it the motto of the Enlightenment philosophers. Your five-year-old can think for herself; she wants to know everything, and she can indeed be daring! This last year before your child embarks on her twelve-year mandatory educational cycle is a coming of age of sorts. In a few short years, your child has grown from helpless infant to capable child. The coming year is an exciting one in which your child's ability to learn and remember will amaze you. In the next chapter we will learn more about the processes that constitute human memory, and the remarkable role music can play in helping to consolidate our memories throughout life. We also will see how children in the sixth year are more equipped than ever before to benefit from exposure to other cultures, ways of thinking, and musical traditions — experiences that will help to make them not only more creative but also more empathetic, and perhaps even happier and more successful as well.

6 YEAR SIX
The Age of Enlightenment

SCAN ME

N JANUARY THE SUN NEVER SEEMS TO FULLY RISE in Paris. The skies are always gray, the streets damp, and everything looks like a black-and-white movie. It is exactly the time of year when you need music the most.

One dark morning I came back to our campus of four- and five-year-olds after an extended trip abroad, excited to return to the bright and colorful world I knew was awaiting me. While I was away, the children had been preparing an opera in Mandarin, "Nian the Dragon," in anticipation of the world premiere. I couldn't wait to see the costumes and props that our talented staff created while I was traveling.

I could hear the children giggling from down the hall. They knew I'd be coming that morning, and that I hadn't yet seen their costumes or the decor. I opened the door and gasped. There were red lanterns everywhere, and in the center of the room, a papier-mâché dragon's head with a cloth "body" under which several children were dancing and giggling. A group of children I recognized as the "hunters" were chanting, *"Duo KAI,"* or "Go away," while playing the rhythm of the words on their coffee can drums. They were eager to show me everything, and began excitedly telling me about the significance of the color red in Chinese culture and explaining that *hongse* is "red" in Mandarin.

Now it was time for the dress rehearsal. One of their teachers took the rambunctious dragon(s) backstage as another guided the hunters to the back of the classroom for their entrance. Once the orchestra — made up of five-year-olds — had taken their places, the curtain closed, and our head teacher clapped her hands together: "Presenting 'Nian the Dragon!'"

When our Mandarin teacher, who wanted the children to learn about Chinese New Year's traditions, had first told me about the festival's colorful origin myth about the dragon named Nian, I suggested that we make an opera about it. According to tradition, Nian (which also means "new year" in Mandarin) was a vicious dragon who terrorized a local village until the townspeople discovered the dragon's Achilles' heel: Nian was afraid of all things red. The townspeople tore up bits of red fabric and waved them at the dragon until it succumbed. The story is the basis of the colorful Chinese New Year's tradition. We wrote a short, simplified version of the story, and I set about writing music for the key Mandarin phrases. Our Mandarin teacher, Xin Li, wrote them out in pinyin — the standardized phonetic transcription of the Mandarin words using the Roman alphabet — and she recorded them as well.

Not speaking any Mandarin myself, I had trouble keeping the Mandarin words in my head; I had to listen to the recordings over and over again until I began to hear the melodic quality of the words. I then tried to make my musical melodies match with their ups and downs. I used a pentatonic scale to make sure that the music sounded non-Western and more authentically Chinese. (The pentatonic scale is the five-note scale that originated in ancient Greece and is frequently used in traditional Chinese music. You can obtain this scale by playing the black notes on a keyboard, beginning with the group of three. If you have ever heard traditional Chinese music, you will instantly recognize this particular scale.)

I had managed to come up with some melodies that stuck in my own head, but the real test, of course, would be to see if the children retained the melodies easily. I was in for quite a surprise.

A month earlier, on the first day the children were introduced to their new Mandarin opera, we told them the story, then we sang the songs together, very dramatically. When we reached the part where the dragon dies, all the children acted out prolonged and agonizing deaths, and we all had a good dark laugh. Then I left them for the morning, which they filled with their usual diet of music, movement, art, and academics.

When it was nearing lunchtime, as the children were putting away their activities and milling about, I heard something. The children were wailing the dying dragon lament, trying to outdo one another in their feigned desperation. They had already retained the words and the melody, not to mention the drama. I was astonished until I realized that I, too, could now remember the words.

In the ensuing weeks, the children continued to ready themselves for the premiere of their opera, to be presented to an audience of highly objective parents. Every day they begged to work on "Nian." It was clear that this format, a story put to music, was something that the children loved. The magic of make-believe was plainly at work.

Since then, we have written two additional operas in Mandarin, but I'll never forget that dreary January morning, as I sat watching the final rehearsal of "Nian the Dragon." I was moved and inspired to see this group of five-year-olds, so deeply involved in the story and so in tune with one another that they seemed oblivious to the fact that they were singing in Mandarin.

The story of "Nian the Dragon" began with a group of village children happily playing the game "rock, scissors, paper" — in Mandarin. Then we heard the dragon's heavy footsteps as it began its ominous march to the stage, chanting in Mandarin, "I'm hungry, I'm going to eat you." The orchestra, seated on the floor, was playing the rhythmic ostinato on drums, xylophones, and wood blocks. (An ostinato is a rhythm that is repeated over and over. It comes from the Latin *obstinatus*, and it is indeed obstinate.)

The village children hugged one another in fear as the dragon approached.

Once the dragon reached the stage, the village children sang, "*Wo bu xiuan nian, whoa haipa*" (I don't like Nian, I'm afraid), as an orchestra member seated on the floor played the lament on a small metal xylophone with a bell-like timbre, giving the melody a particularly haunting quality.

The dragon continued to stomp his feet chanting, "*Wo EUH le, wo EUH le. wo CHEU nimen, wo CHEU nimen*" (I'm hungry, I'm going to eat you). Then, from the back of the room, the hunters, who were tapping chopsticks on coffee can drums hanging from their necks, intoned, "*Duo kai!*" They got louder and louder, drumming and stomping as they reached the stage. The narrator stepped in, lamenting in English, "What a mess, we could really use some wisdom."

This was the cue for the wise people — the Sages — to enter, gently swinging their red lanterns and singing, "*Wo xihuan hongse,*" or "I love red." They offered little pieces of red cloth to everyone, and they began to encircle Nian while waving their red rags. The dragon sang, "I'm afraid of red, I'm afraid of fire."

The dragon was meant to slowly slide to the floor and perish, but the dragon in our rehearsal was dancing and giggling, visibly enjoying itself, not in the least bit afraid. The narrator had to insist several times, saying louder and louder, "And Nian slowly slid to the ground and perished."

Finally the dragon slid to the floor, and the other children encircled the lifeless body while the dragon children snuck out from under their costume and exited backstage. The circle of children then opened up, and little Constance lifted the dragon costume delicately and whispered, "*Nian pow le,*" or "Nian has disappeared!" Another child whispered, "*Nian pow le,*" and the news spread like wildfire in our imaginary Chinese village.

Soon the children were singing a celebratory, highly rhythmic "*Nian pow le*" and dancing joyously. This marked the end of the opera, and thus the end of our rehearsal, so I clapped and whooped my appreciation — but the children had no intention of stopping. Meanwhile, the dragons reentered and joined in the dancing, as did we all. Finally we had to call an end to this, to the dismay of the children. It was lunchtime.

LANGUAGE, MUSIC, AND MEMORY

The children's immersion in the "Nian the Dragon" opera involves phonetic, rhythmic, melodic, and tonal sensitivity, and almost immediate memorization. Their experience shows how effectively music can serve as a support system for language acquisition, and, more broadly, opens a window onto the mysterious interplay between language, music, and memory. This is the "overlap" in Patel's OPERA hypothesis. It is also a fascinating real-life example of the rapid memorization and retention of an entirely new and extremely foreign language at a very young age, a process stimulated and accelerated by music.

Not only had the children memorized the opera's complicated (and for the most part entirely foreign) phrases, but also they were manipulating the subtle variations in tone that determine the meaning of Mandarin words. Melody, rhythm, movement, and pleasure facilitated a task that most adult learners find incredibly daunting.

Mandarin is a *tonal* language, which means that the way you raise or lower your voice when speaking a syllable changes the meaning entirely. The classic textbook illustration of the four tones of Mandarin uses the syllable *ma*. Imagine all the different ways of saying *ma*. Depending on how you pronounce it, it means, respectively, "mother," "hemp," "horse," or "scolding."

Mandarin Tones

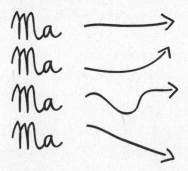

ma — your voice is perfectly flat: mother

ma — your voice goes up like a question: hemp

ma — your voice wiggles in between, going down then swooping back up: horse

ma — your voice goes sharply down like a negative order: a reproach

Perhaps unsurprisingly, researchers have found that children who speak a tonal language and practice music have extremely advanced pitch recognition. A very high percentage of Mandarin-speaking children who practice music have perfect pitch. But perfect pitch is not the goal here; the goal is to develop pitch *recognition*. This is not just because pitch recognition is important for musical practice (although it is), but also because, as we have seen in the previous chapter, language and music both involve sound recognition. The more precise a child's ability to distinguish sounds, the better they can detect language subtleties. Advanced musical ability, or excellent pitch recognition, has been determined to be a critical factor in literacy and also in second-language acquisition.

In addition to being a remarkable example of language learning, the Mandarin opera story illustrates the profound effects of musical practice in terms of cooperation, coordination, and cohesion — three of the benefits highlighted by Stefan Koelsch, as I described in chapter 2. Indeed, the children who were rehearsing the Nian opera were practically sailing the "7 Cs." They were waiting their turns, coordinating their bodies and voices, and helping one another out. They were working together for a common goal: the creation of a story with music. The children in our little opera were synchronized, inside and out; not only were they playing, singing, and dancing together, but also they were anticipating what needed to happen next.

The entire experience was so pleasurable for them that months, even years, later the children burst into songs from this opera at the mention of dragons, or *hongse,* and especially upon hearing a pentatonic scale. It is rare to see an elaborately choreographed musical production in a foreign language with children this age, not because they are incapable, but because adults often underestimate this age group and the degree of stimulation they crave. But these five-year-olds can accomplish so much musically and linguistically if we give them a chance.

A little-known fact about our brain is that it begins "pruning" very early in life — shedding those neural connections that it doesn't use often so that it can focus on those it uses the most. If a child is exposed to three languages, for example, the brain will maintain sensitivity to all three, but if one of the languages disappears from the child's environment, the brain slowly loses interest. Likewise, exposure to only one kind of music — "children's music," for instance, or Western music — makes us what scientists call "culture-bound." Passive exposure to limited forms of music will reduce the genres and styles with which a child feels comfortable, and thus might want to reproduce. This creates an unnecessary limitation. We really can go global with our youngest children, and improvisation of many different kinds of music can and should play a major part in their experience.

The implications of being culture-bound (or unbound, as it were) are greater than simply one's musical choices. The level of empathy that people feel for one another often depends on whether or not they see themselves as belonging to a group together, and a group can be defined or constrained by what its members do or do not share. When we expand those parameters, we increase the possibility of becoming part of a larger, more inclusive group. Think about widened musical and linguistic exposure in this context. The goal is not to make a show of the child's musical awareness and extensive vocabulary but simply to avoid becoming "culture-bound." The wider one's linguistic, cultural, and musical horizons are, the deeper one's creative reflection will be, and the more one will perceive things as being familiar and nonthreatening.

It seems likely that memory, too, can benefit from becoming unstuck from our particular cultural niche. To wit: in late June of the same year that we produced the Nian opera at L'École Koenig, we saw a remarkable example of long-term retention and effortless memory retrieval involving a tiny little girl and a dragon.

Rheanne was not yet three when we were working on the opera. The class of the youngest children had learned a slightly simplified version of "Nian." At the end of the school year, five months after the premiere, I made an appointment to say good-bye to her family. It was late afternoon, and some of the children from the after-school program were playing with me at the piano, so I didn't see Rheanne's family come in. I was improvising with two children in a Do pentatonic scale when suddenly Rheanne, who had entered the room with her parents, burst into song, belting out the dying dragon lament.

I was astonished. This child had just turned three. No one could have been playing this little song for her in the intervening months, as no one had the music, and there was not yet a recording. She had heard the tonality (the pentatonic scale in Do), and the flood-gates of her personal river of music, memory, and emotion opened up. The music and words sprang out of her. Rheanne had, between January and June, learned many other songs, in many different languages — and yet she remembered the dragon lament, and sang it, perfectly.

After impressing us with this display, Rheanne of course wanted to sing all the songs from the opera next, as well as every song that she had learned that year. Such is the power that music has in our memories — a power that is fundamental to the very architecture of memory itself.

MUSIC, MEMORY, AND SELF

Not surprisingly, research on our specific memory for music suggests that the key determinants of long-term memory for song (both music and words) are the degree of positive emotion experienced and the age at which the song is learned. Studies show that the music we have heard at a specific moment in our life is strongly linked to our autobiographical memory — the bank of memories that make up our sense of self, and which begins forming very early in life.

Take the example of little Rheanne. I'm quite sure that her emotional experience of enacting the dragon's death was positive, in spite of the scene's morbid nature. For her, this was a song she loved to sing and a role she loved to play, in a group to which she loved to belong. Rheanne's début as an opera star at age two and a half has most certainly become a part of a very positive autobiographical memory. No one can say if she will remember this song later in life, but we do know that early positive personal memories become part of what makes us secure and confident throughout life.

Memory is a complex, invisible phenomenon that determines who we are in our deepest inner selves. To understand human behavior, cognition, and development, we first need to understand memory. When we fall in love, what do we want to share? Our memories. What do we want to learn about our loved one? Their past, their memories, everything that makes them the unique object of our fascination. The intoxication of falling in love is often relived through a favorite piece of music, "our song." Decades later, many of us will still feel a stab of emotion upon hearing that particular song. (When the study of memory began long ago in ancient Greece, its founders may have had some inkling of this. Aristotle's "On Memory and Reminiscence" attributed memory to the human soul and located it in the human heart. Perhaps this is why we still use the phrase "learn it by heart" when we speak of memorization.)

Of course, memory formation happens in the brain, not in the heart — although the precise mechanics of this process are still being studied. In 1968, the cognitive scientists Richard Atkinson and Richard Shiffrin from Stanford University proposed a new theory of this cognitive process, called the Multi-Store Model of Memory, which identified clearly defined paths and divisions of memory types.

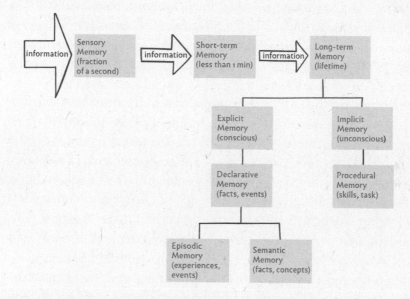

The process begins in our bodies, via our senses. Our bodies provide sensory information that passes through our short-term memory corridor before either disappearing or moving down the path into our long-term memory. Atkinson and Shiffrin believed that short-term memory becomes long-term memory (LTM) through rehearsal or repetition. Without this repetition, the memory will never take root in the brain, and will simply evaporate. Here, perhaps, lies the root of the power and durability of musical memories.

Think of the quantity of input our senses take in every day—all the sounds, feelings, words, and images. According to Atkinson and Shiffrin, only those that are consciously revisited will enter into the long-term memory store. Someone can give you a phone number on a slip of paper, but your memorization process is enhanced when you say it out loud. With enough practice, the phone number lands in the LTM store, on the left side of the diagram, down in the semantic (facts, concepts, and words) area. Motor skills, such as tying our shoelaces, move to the right side of the LTM store, into the procedural memory (automatisms) store. A fond memory from our first-grade classroom will move to our episodic memory, the part of the storage room where we keep our personal stories.

The Atkinson-Shiffrin model continues to have relevance, but advances in neuroscience have added considerable nuance. Increasingly research is turning to the impact of emotions in the memory process. At one conference I attended, a scientist played a very simple game with the audience to demonstrate the impact of emotion on memory encoding. "Can you remember what you did Wednesday afternoon three weeks ago?" There was a small, tentative show of hands. Then she asked, "Can you remember what you were doing during the morning of September 11, 2001?" The entire audience raised their hands.

Studies have also confirmed what musicians have always known: musical memory involves both implicit and explicit memory centers. When we make music, we are relying on our implicit procedural memory, which allows us to play our instruments without any conscious effort. When we are learning a new piece of music, however, we are consciously thinking about what we are playing.

Explicit memory is conscious and requires an effort. Implicit memory is unconscious, or automatic. Implicit memory therefore is very much a part of our long-term memory. A part of our implicit memory involves motor skills, those required for bicycle riding, swimming, and playing an instrument. This memory requires no further rehearsal once established, and it never goes away. Our motor skills are part of the subcategory of implicit memory called procedural memory. Music is stored in this part of our LTM because we use motor skills to play music or to dance. The years of practice necessary to develop instrumental mastery also develop this robust "automatic" physical ability (procedural memory), and once it is in place, it stays.

If you play an instrument, it's easy to see how deep implicit memory is. Many musicians can go to a piano and begin playing a piece they learned early in life, with no effort or even thought. I have experienced this firsthand, finding myself playing a piece of music learned long ago that my fingers appear to know, while I have no idea what the name of the piece is. Very quickly, however, semantic and episodic memory kick in, and the name of the music, the composer, or the context in which I learned it will resurface.

This is a perfect example of the implicit-explicit waltz that many musicians (and athletes) experience. After years of practice, I no longer need to think about how to play a melody on my instrument; I rely on my implicit memory. If I am playing a new piece of music, however, or if I am improvising, my explicit memory is in high gear while my procedural (implicit) memory is calmly cruising along. Music enters our brain through so many portals that preservation in our LTM is almost inevitable. For instance, we cannot make music without our body being involved. Even when we are only listening, some part of our body is moving, voluntarily or involuntarily. Unlike speech, which has specific treatment centers in our brain, music has no one dedicated operations center. When people are placed in an fMRI scanner while playing or singing, we see multiple areas of their brain lighting up, indicating that they are *all* involved. Robert Zatorre, a cognitive neuroscientist at the Montreal Neurological Institute of McGill University and co-director of the International Laboratory for Brain Music and Sound Research (BRAMS), has a delightful way of expressing this. When asked where music is processed in the brain, he replied, "Not everybody agrees with my point of view, but I like to say when I'm asked that question that the part of the brain that handles music is everything from the neck up."

The precise trajectory of musical processing in our memory system has not yet been clearly identified. One of the avenues being investigated is the possibility that musical memory may differ from semantic (word) memory. Music may enter our audio system and move to our short-term memory through a different door than speech. This means that singing something and saying something engage the brain in different ways.

What if we took this hypothesis and applied it to the Mandarin opera? As the children repetitively practice singing and dancing their new songs, the Mandarin words they are using are making their way down to the semantic LTM store. The words are also joined with the melodies, rhythms, and movements that waltz through the children's short-term memory corridor, into the procedural memory store. This is where the proverbial "bicycle riding" memory lives — the type of memory that never goes away. The rhythm, melodies, and movements of the children's opera experience channeled the meaning and the emotional impact of the foreign phrases into that deep and durable part of their memory system. In this way, learning can take place much faster and more indelibly than we could have imagined — especially with Mandarin, a language that shares almost nothing with the languages the children already spoke.

Although we cannot single out a specific element in music that is responsible for facilitating language retention, we know that rhythm, melody, movement, repetition, and emotion combine to make musical memories some of our most surprising. This is charmingly demonstrated in travel experiences that many of us have had. I remember a taxi driver in Egypt singing me Michael Jackson's "Billie Jean" even though he did not speak a word of English. Musicians and non-musicians alike have all experienced the phenomenon I call the *mysterious melody*. We begin humming a tune, then start singing the words without any recall effort. The mysterious melody is an example of implicit memory because we don't really know where the song is coming from. The answer is most certainly that without being aware, we experienced a "trigger," something that brings the memory instantly to the surface.

In Rheanne's case, the trigger was the pentatonic scale. Presumably the Do pentatonic scale had become part of Rheanne's implicit memory, not with the label of Do pentatonic but with the powerful feeling of "dragon music." As soon as she heard the pentatonic scale, the dragon lament leaped up from her memory, and she spontaneously gave it voice. Many educators would not consider this possible in three-year-olds, but we have learned that very young children have incredible tonal recognition and retention.

Music provides a lifelong emotional outlet, a means of expressing our complex feelings of joy, longing, or nostalgia. Music is one of the principal triggers of nostalgia, along with taste and smell. Music can create the feeling of nostalgia, but music is also our go-to choice when we want to call up this bittersweet emotion.

THE POWER OF MUSICAL MEMORY

The science of musical memory is continuing to evolve, but as we have seen, music does appear to aid with the creation of memories of all types. And its power in this regard — which stems from a combination of positive emotion, song, movement, and ear training in early childhood — opens up exciting possibilities for the creative use of music, whether it is in learning foreign languages or multiplication tables, in storytelling or reading. But sometimes the memory-supporting uses to which people put music are amazing enough already.

Pierre began in our school when he was three. He completed our preschool program, and after graduation, he began at a Parisian primary school with no music program. We encouraged his parents to continue musical practice for Pierre, so one of our music teachers started weekly piano lessons with him. I checked in regularly on his progress because he had been exceptionally fluent in the language of music. His teacher told me amusing stories of how he would send Pierre out of the room and play hide-and-seek games with him, challenging him to guess not only individual notes but chords and scales as well. Pierre loved these games, and he was very good at them.

Pierre was progressing well on the piano, but he was experiencing emotional difficulties in the context of a complicated family situation. His teacher told me that Pierre would sometimes, out of the blue, begin playing some of the melodies from his preschool years. His teacher had not taught him these tunes; Pierre had "found" them himself. He asked his teacher over and over again to teach him these songs. He wanted to learn the songs with both hands — all of the songs from his early childhood. It was clear to the teacher that Pierre was seeking solace in the music he had learned during a happier time. He was nostalgic for that time, and music was his preferred emotional outlet.

One day Pierre, who was now ten, asked his teacher to play him his "musical name," a motif that he had not heard for years. His teacher played it for him, and then on a whim asked if he would like to play "Guess Who?" with the musical names of his former classmates. Not only did Pierre recognize his own "name," but also he recognized the musical names of all of his former classmates. In the case of one little boy who had left the school after only a year, Pierre said that he could not remember the boy's name but that he had brown hair and droopy eyes, and that he had moved away. His teacher asked, "Do you mean Oscar?" Pierre nodded yes: Oscar! Even though Pierre could not summon up the boy's name, he remembered the music! His deep musical memory was intact and stronger than his semantic (word) memory.

Music has been known to support memory in even stranger and more unusual circumstances. One of the most poignant examples of this involves the Vietnam War and the song "Old MacDonald Had a Farm."

During an air raid one night in 1966, a freshly enlisted twenty-year-old American navy private named Douglas Hegdahl snuck onto the deck of his ship to get a better look. Somehow in the commotion, he fell overboard. Hegdahl swam for twelve hours before being found by Cambodian fishermen, who eventually handed him over to the North Vietnamese. Hegdahl became an inmate in the notorious Hoa Lo prison, nicknamed the "Hanoi Hilton." It was there that he began an incredibly original counterespionage campaign — one drawn entirely from the power of musical memory.

His North Vietnamese jailers were convinced that Hegdahl was CIA, and when he denied it, the beatings began. So Hegdahl decided to play dumb — very dumb. Reading anti-American propaganda material was regularly demanded of the prisoners of war, and when they refused, they were beaten to the brink of death. Hegdahl, however, graciously obliged his tormentors, but added, in his best country drawl, "Of course, y'all, only one li'l problem: I can't read."

What did his captors do? They got him a tutor, and when this failed, presuming that his eyesight was the root of his problem, they got him eyeglasses. This involved taking him to Hanoi several times.

During these trips, Hegdahl memorized the route to the prison.

The eyeglasses did not help, and Hegdahl was so convincing in his role of an illiterate dimwit that his captors began calling him "the incredibly stupid one." As a result, Hegdahl was given free range of the prison and started secretly collecting information and acting as a runner among the other POWs.

Unaware of Hegdahl's activities, the North Vietnamese decided to release him after two years. He was one of the first returning POWs of the Vietnam War. And when he returned, he brought something enormous with him.

Hegdahl had memorized the names and pertinent information of 256 prisoners of war incarcerated with him in the Hanoi Hilton. Upon release, he communicated all their names to the US government, and for the first time in years, the families of these men learned that their sons, brothers, and husbands were alive.

How did he memorize all those names? By putting them to music — to the tune of "Old MacDonald."

To this day, Hegdahl can still sing the names of all 256 men. He committed the names to long-term memory by encoding them through rhythmic and melodic repetition. Hegdahl could only recite the names if he sang the song and if he sang it fast. The bemused higher-ups who debriefed him would ask him to slow down, but he couldn't.

Today we know why Hegdahl had to stick to his tempo: he had memorized the names with the same song, at the same tempo, day after day, until they had become part of his procedural, automatic memory. In this way they became implicit — just like muscle memory for a guitar player.

When combined, rhythm and melody are powerful allies in memory retention. In preceding chapters we learned how the building blocks of both melody and rhythm skills (pitch recognition and rhythmic training) can become part of our implicit memory if introduced early in life,

The visual equivalent of pitch recognition — or the ability to distinguish one musical note from another — is identifying color and shape. We teach children that the color they perceive has a name, "red." We point to a shape and assign it a name, "square." With a few repetitions this information moves into long-term memory, specifically the implicit part of our LTM. We never have to think about it again. Most people will draw a blank if you ask them how they know that red is red. The same goes for people with excellent pitch recognition; they won't be able to explain how they know that a La is a La.

For some reason, we clearly trust what we see more than what we hear, and so spend a lot more time teaching children to recognize colors than teaching them to sing and name pitches. And yet hearing is fully functional at birth, and even the youngest children have the capacity to fine-tune their aural skills. The fluency they develop will dance itself into their long-term memory. The sooner we start to teach them to recognize pitches, the better.

We already do this with language. Linguists consider the knowledge of grammar and syntax to be examples of implicit memory because both are learned before we become aware of the learning. Later in life, we learn the names of the grammatical structures that we already effortlessly employ in our speech. Learning the rules of grammar is not part of our native language learning experience, because this experience is purely oral. Children learn through trial, error, experimentation, and encouragement. We don't tell our children, "Honey, you're mixing up your personal pronouns again."

Pitch, rhythm, and musical syntax, like grammar, can also become part of our implicit memory through early exposure, especially if it is on par with early childhood exposure to language. The musical equivalent of grammatical syntax is musical form. One basic example of this is the tradition of beginning and ending a simple piece of music on the same note. As we saw in chapter 5, this gives us a sense of "going home." A more sophisticated musical form is the sonata form from the classical era. Sonata form consists of the introduction of a theme, a development, a recapitulation, and sometimes a coda (an ending to the piece with new material). The last note of the piece has indeed "resolved to the tonic," and is held longer, clearly indicating the end. You may remember the startling resemblance of this musical form to the twenty-seven-second mother-baby exchange that we saw in chapter 1. Whether musical forms came from language or the other way around, they are both part of what we absorb very early in life, most of the time unconsciously. We now know that grammar and syntax are something children need to absorb before the age of seven; otherwise their speech will never be completely fluent. I believe we can achieve a high level of musical expertise if we bring an interactive (musicking) experience to children during the same period in which they are absorbing language.

THE MUSICAL ACCELERATOR

Musicking in early life, even learning to recognize pitches, is not about winning the intelligence race. The goal is to give children access to a meta-language that will allow them to communicate with others on a level deeper than language. As if that weren't enough, music also enhances language processing — both with our mother tongues and with foreign languages. And as we have seen previously, music helps in basic literacy — beginning with speech, which leads to reading.

Although science has determined that children need to understand how to break down words, proponents of the "global method" still insist that reading develops naturally through exposure to writing and books. In spite of a report commissioned by National Educational Systems, published in 2000, clearly indicating that the phonetic approach to reading achieves superior results, the phonetic reading system is still not fully in place and does not figure as mandatory training for teachers.

To help children learn how to read, teachers and parents should keep in mind that a child needs to be able to hear a sound before they can be asked to recognize a letter. I cannot insist enough, if a child does not hear the difference between the sound of a *b* and the sound of a *p*, we ought to start there. Orality first — always. This is where music is a powerful ally.

For our eager five-year-olds, ready to start the process of learning to read, I began to imagine how a song could teach children the letter sounds. It would have to involve engaging music, dancing, and humor to make phonetic learning fun instead of annoying.

It ended up taking three months and a great staff to finalize our bilingual phonics song. The melody came quite quickly, but finding the right words for the sounds the children needed to learn was quite a challenge, especially in two languages. At some point during our last heated discussion about "urchins" as opposed to "unicorns," "iguanas" as opposed to "inchworms," I almost threw in the towel. Then finally the moment came to try out our new song and dance with the children.

In the song, each letter of the alphabet has quirky, therefore memorable, lyrics, with repetition of the letter sound (not the letter name) and its own choreography. A flashcard shows the letter, the lyrics, and a funny illustration of the movement involved. We tried it out in both languages, French and English, for the first time during a morning circle. Not only did the children join in immediately, but also, as the day went on, we heard bits of the song popping up: "Dinosaurs are dancing," or "Beautiful balloons." The dinosaurs were especially popular because the children go down on all fours and kick up their hind legs. The next morning, the first thing they wanted to do was learn more of their phonics song. We were creating a positive implicit memory in those receptive young brains. This was phonetic learning supercharged by melody, rhythm, vision, and movement. The dopamine was visibly kicking in, and the children experienced only happiness.

Scientists are uncharacteristically unanimous about multimodal learning — the style of learning epitomized by this exercise. When we take in information through multiple portals, with some element of emotional engagement, we increase the likelihood of deep and permanent learning. Even our youngest children learn to recognize and memorize both the sounds and feelings of letters through their song, and they love it.

Of course, this is not the only way that music can help children learn how to read and write. As I mentioned in chapter 2, the vestibular system — the sensory system that gives us our sense of balance and spatial orientation — is crucial for allowing children to perform these basic academic skills. That is because the vestibular system helps children keep their eyes focused while their bodies move (which our bodies are always doing, however imperceptibly). Music and movement are essential nutrients for growing vestibular systems starting in the earliest years of a child's life — a developmental phase that helps lay the groundwork for academic success later on.

In the course of exploring the link between sound, language, music, emotion, and embodied cognition, our teachers and I have arrived at an important conclusion: music should become part of a curriculum not only for musical and prosocial purposes but also for academic learning acceleration. We began to fantasize about teaching *everything* through music! If we could use it to teach language, for instance, why couldn't we use it to teach math?

Singing and Dancing the Phonetic Alphabet

Ants on an anthill Ah ah ah

Beautiful balloons Buh buh buh

Cats are coughing Cuh cuh cuh

Dinosaurs are dancing Duh duh duh

Ants on an anthill Ah ah ah
Beautiful balloons Buh buh buh
Cats are coughing Cuh cuh cuh
Dinosaurs are dancing Duh duh duh

When your child sings this song, singing the sound of the letter, not the name, while making the movements and looking at the funny images, she is activating five different memory modes: semantic, melodic, rhythmic, sensorial, and visual. Once you have sung these four letters in order a number of times, try mixing up the cards for fun. The most important thing is that your child associates the image of the letter with the sound the letter makes — the wide-open *Ah* and the "hard" consonants *Buh, Cuh,* and *Duh.*

Beginning readers need to sound out letters, but not in the Greek alpha, beta, gamma, delta order to which we've grown accustomed. There are varying opinions about which letters should be introduced first, but most specialists agree on the necessity of introducing *A, C, S, P, I,* and *T* (SATPIN) to start with in English. For simplicity's sake, we will bring in the letter *T* directly after the first four letters. Sing and dance this one several times as well.

A Tiger under a table Tuhtuh tuhtuh

a tiger under a table

You can spend a lot of time playing with the letter sounds before moving on to actual words. If your child does not immediately sing "Dinosaurs are dancing" when he sees the d-dinosaur flashcard, keep shuffling the cards and singing and dancing the individual letters. When you sense this is solid, you can move on to combining the sounds.

Put your "Cats are coughing" card on the floor and sing the melody with the movements. Place the "Ants on anthill" card on the floor next to it. Sing the C melody again, insisting on the hard C. Then sing the A melody again, insisting on the short A sound. Ask your child what happens when you put them together. French children love this because *caca* means poopoo!

Now ask your child to close her eyes and place the *T* card on the floor. It's a word, and you are both going to learn to read it. Begin by singing the sound of each letter: *cuh cuh cuh, ah ah ah, tuh tuh tuh;* now one time only: *cu, ah, tuh.* Ask your child to squish the sounds together. Even if she needs a little help at first, that *CAT* is going to jump out of the cards in no time!

MUSIC FOR MATH

After the success of the alphabet song, I decided to write a skip counting rap song for children to learn to memorize their multiplication tables. I loved the idea of the children literally skipping across the room while rapping.

Skip Counting Rap

Children have all heard an intoxicating rap beat, and most children love it! This game draws on the power of rhythm and movement to create implicit memory, allowing children to retain their multiplication tables remarkably quickly. This is only the tens rap, the first table that children learn. The same format is used for fives and twos.

I've got a game that I'd like to share with you
doo ba ba doo baba dooba dooba dooooooo

. . .

We're going to skip count and that's a lot of fun
jumpin and bumpin we're really on a run

. . .

Are you ready? Um. Take a deep breath and

. . .

ten twenty thirty forty fifty you won!
— we can go further — it's so much fun!

. . .

ten twenty thirty forty fifty and
sixty seventy eighty ninety
Yo! One hundred you won! —
counting in tens is so much fun!

Now that you and your child have got the song down, it's time to get moving. The children get to dip with their legs and wave their arms during the beginning of the song, but they aren't allowed to jump until the numbers begin. Ideally they should jump over approximately equal distances. For some children (and adults), hopping with both feet is challenging, so rather than interrupt the rhythm, hop on alternate feet. Once the children know what's coming, they can hardly wait for the moment when they can begin to hop across the room or the driveway! If you are feeling daringly multimodal, you or your child can also draw the numbers in chalk on a sidewalk, the driveway, or the floor. Try rewinding or going backwards, both the numbers and the jumping. This rap and dance always ends up with everybody rolling with laughter.

The only problem with the skip counting rap in tens was that the children learned it too quickly. We had to scramble and come up with the next multiplication tables very quickly, adapting the rap for fives, then twos. This was an exciting period in the history of the school. Parents were telling us that their children were teaching them the multiplications rap. The children were also teaching the alphabet song to their parents, making sure that they mastered the movements, like Maxime had done with his Baby Musicking lesson. When learning is playful and fun, children blossom, and they want to share their pleasure with their families.

There have been many claims over the past few decades about a possible relationship between music and math fluency, and often these are simply media misdemeanors: for instance, to explode the most basic of these neuromyths, it is not because a child practices music that she becomes gifted in math. In fact, recent research has indicated that musical expertise does not automatically transfer to other areas. It is not because your child has musical training that she will automatically excel in math, science, or any other field.

With that said, there *is* an organic relationship between rhythm and math that can be experienced in the body, and which can help children improve their mathematical skills through musical exercises of the sort I provide in what follows. Rhythm naturally helps children fine-tune their motor skills. They learn to stomp and clap to a beat and learn to do so at many different speeds or "tempi." Rhythm training can lead to a visceral understanding of proportion, division, multiplication, and maybe even the concept of infinity. Understanding proportions (the relationship of a part to the whole) is a prelude to understanding fractions; when this concept is properly introduced, young children grasp it immediately. After all, what child is not interested in the proportion of the cake left for her once her siblings have been served?

Our Magic Musical Apple story taps into this relationship. It's not a demonstration of music releasing mathematical genius, nor an example of a transferal process. This is validation that rhythm and math share certain elements, and rhythm can function as the entry portal for math because it is experienced in the body.

This is a variation on the Wicked Woodsperson game from chapter 4. In class, we ask the children to sing "*ro-o-on-de*" and "one-two-three-four" while they pass an apple to one another, making a circle with the apple in the air. We then cut the apple in half so there are two pieces — two *blanches* or half notes. With another swipe of the knife we have four pieces — *noires* or quarter notes. The children get to scream each time the knife cuts into the apple, which cranks up the collective emotional volume level several notches.

When we get to eighth notes or *croches*, the children are happily fluttering the four fingers of both hands and chirping at the same time: *"Croche croche croche croche."* (*Croc-croche* means "bite into the eighth note.") With the youngest children, we give them the apple pieces to eat, and we all sing *"croc-croche, croc-croche"* while they gobble up their eighth notes.

With the older children, we begin to speak about "twice as small" and "twice as big," leading to "twice as fast" and "twice as slow." The children know that the *ronde* lasts twice as long as the *blanche*. They feel this in their bodies as they make the movements, and they hear it when they sing *"ro-o-on-de"* and *"blan-che."* Now they see the physical size of the apple slices: the whole becomes a half before their eyes, and they instantly make the connection.

With the older children, we then reconstruct the apple, establishing a link between rhythm and proportions. We speak of *blanches* and halves, of *noires* and quarters, and the *ronde* as a whole. The children think they are chopping up and piecing together an apple; we know that we are consolidating their rhythm skills and also learning about proportions.

This is bottom-up learning at its best. The children are not memorizing facts or concepts; they are feeling when something lasts for four beats or two beats — twice as long, half as long. To make the leap to twice as big or twice as small is a piece of cake (or apple).

The Magic Musical Apple is one of the children's favorite games. Your child is likely to ask for this game every day, and all the better. The more she plays this game, the deeper her sense of time, size, and proportion will become. All you need to do this exercise at home, once you have read the classroom story, is an apple, a knife, and a flair for drama. If your experience matches ours, your child will enjoy this so much that you're going to want to have a lot of apples on hand!

Ta o-o-o   Ta-o   Ta

Sit down with your child, an apple, a chopping block, and a knife. Remember that you are a human metronome; you will need to keep the beat by gently rocking from side to side during the entire exercise. Remember that tempo (speed) is important: don't rock too slowly — you and your child need to be moving in synchrony. Keep in mind that the fractions used to name rhythms in many parts of the world are impossible for young children because the syllables don't match the rhythm. There are some excellent systems for rhythm training that involve the use of matching syllables. One of the best is from the renowned Kodály method. You can use these syllables or the French nomenclature discussed earlier.

> *The whole note is "Ta-o-o-o,"*
> *The half note is "Ta-o,"*
> *The quarter note is "Ta."*

Take the apple in both hands and lift it with a circular motion in front of you, singing either *"ro-o-on-de"* or "Ta-o-o-o." Alternate between one or both of these and actual counting: "one, two, three, four." Your child will join you as soon as she has heard this once, and then she is going to want the apple herself. It's her turn now to lift the apple in the air; keep singing with her, and you may need to guide her through all four beats because slow and long are challenging for young children. Once this is in place, the fun will begin:

"What are we going to do now?"

"Chop it in half!"

With excruciating drama, chop the apple in two and give the two halves to your child — all the while singing *"blan-che,"* "Ta-o," and "one-two." She needs to hold up each hand one after the other, singing the syllables. Now reiterate the drama and cut each half in half again. Holding four items is tricky, so you can each take two pieces and sing *"noire-noire noire-noire,"* "Ta-ta ta-ta," or "one, one, one, one." Keep gently rocking in time with your words.

Now it's time to glue the apple back together. Make this into a guessing game: "What happens if we glue the *'noires'* back together again?" You can wave an invisible magic wand while you put the pieces together, saying, "Abracadabra . . . *blan-che,"* or "Ta-o you shall become!" Repeat the *"blan-che"* movement, holding the reconstituted halves in both hands. Now for the most exciting part. Ask your child to close her eyes and intone, "Abracadabra," *"Ro-o-on-de,"* or "Ta-o-o-o you shall become once more." Put all four pieces back together and place them in your child's cupped hands. You won't have to ask her to open her eyes.

You will see if you try this with your child, no further explanation is really necessary. They get it because they feel it. The sensation and the subsequent understanding then consolidate into implicit memory, both procedural and semantic. This means that when a child studies division later on, she will already have a physical memory of what "half" and "whole" feel like. She will also have a lovely feeling of confidence and security because these concepts were first instilled through music and enjoyment, from the bottom up.

MUSIC AND MEMORY FOR LIFE

The entry portal for all learning, hence all memory, is through one of the body's five senses. One of the most famous scenes in all French literature, in Marcel Proust's *À la Recherche du Temps Perdu* (In Search of Lost Time), involves the involuntary surge of memories triggered by the taste of a little butter muffin, or madeleine. The sensory experience of the madeleine opens the floodgates of memory, bringing Proust's childhood vividly back to him for a fleeting moment.

This widely read scene is so evocative that the "madeleine moment" has become recognizable shorthand for talking about nostalgic memory. How is it that we have failed to make the obvious connection and created educational systems that ignore how such memories are created in early life? We know that music can accelerate foreign language learning and enhance our long-term memory in multiple memory stores. Music reinforces our important episodic and semantic memories. But chiefly, music encodes information in our deep procedural memory, our most profound and indelible memory center. This is the memory that structures our lives: it is resilient, reliable, and the last to go when other parts of our mind begin to fade. Why would we not harness the energy that music provides to this deep and robust memory center?

Music enriches learning in all areas because it involves emotion, sensation, and movement. Musical practice brings young children together in ways that boost confidence, unleash imagination and creativity, reward inquisitiveness, and — perhaps most importantly — spark joy. When children make music together in a group, they are learning to come together with those around them into a cohesive whole. Personally, I feel the most profound gratitude and satisfaction knowing that the children who have come through our schools have their first deep experience of human society as part of an orchestra. In the twenty-first century, is there any more important lesson for them to learn?

CONCLUSION

W E ARE ALL STRUGGLING TO PREPARE OUR children for a future that will be complex, unstable, and filled with exponential change. Climate change, pandemics, species extinction, human migration, and artificial intelligence are going to alter our children's worlds in ways that make current education models almost laughable in their reliance on ideas and beliefs that science has largely disproved. The skills that education specialists and philosophers consider essential today include working collaboratively with others, creative problem solving, and transferring knowledge from one field to another. Sadly, most of the schools that are integrating these considerations are available to only the wealthiest families on the planet. For the rest of us, there is "EdTech." Education technology is all the rage in schools today, but on its own it will be insufficient for preparing children for the greatest challenges they will need to meet in the decades ahead.

The OECD has amassed data on school systems all over the world via its international testing program, the PISA project — and it has discovered that EdTech might be having the opposite effect from what educators intend. PISA, the Program for International Student Assessment, tests fifteen-year-old students from all over the world every three years in reading, mathematics, science, and, more recently, problem-solving skills. PISA findings indicate that children who use computers regularly in school do *worse* in their PISA assessments, regardless of whether they come from privilege or poverty. Perhaps an even more disconcerting finding has been that technology does not bridge the achievement gap between privileged and non-privileged students, as its creators promised it would.

The PISA results confirm this unfortunate truth: there is no significant improvement in student achievement in countries that have chosen to invest in technology. Worse, precious time in these children's lives was also lost. So if not technology, what modes of education should parents and educators be focusing on — and how?

The OECD has concluded that basic literacy and mathematical skills remain the defining elements in the creation of social equality. Children who do not read with absolute ease will struggle both inside and outside of school. Math is more than just adding and subtracting; math teaches children procedure and logic. All over the world, children who read and calculate with ease move through their education cycles smoothly and, we can hope, with pleasure.

We have seen how closely these essential capabilities are aligned with music. Music can fine-tune children's language abilities through pre-reading aural training. Rhythmic practice sets the body and mind up for an instinctive understanding of basic mathematical functions. Music is a mega-powerful learning tool when we know how to harness the energy. We have the research. We just have to get out of the "I'm not musical" rut, or worse, the "music is a pleasant pastime" mindset.

In order to meet the challenges of our brave new world, our societal models are going to need to change — and drastically. And in order to not just survive but also thrive in this new environment, our children are going to need to find meaning and happiness in new ways. I sincerely believe that music holds the key.

It is time to get back to our musical roots — to begin living and working together as an orchestra. The word itself comes from the ancient Greek *orkh stra*, which in turn came from *orkheisthai,* "to dance." Earlier Sanskrit and Proto-Indo-European roots include the notions of *rising up* and *flow*. I cannot think of a better metaphor for physical, emotional, and intellectual collaboration — exactly the kinds of skills that will carry our children through the twenty-first century and into the twenty-second. And if we want to see what such an idea might look like in practice, we don't have far to look.

"El Sistema," a project undertaken in Venezuela, is a beautiful example of an educational system that managed to bridge socioeconomic gaps and bring deep cultural learning and connection to several generations of Venezuelans. Formerly the National Network of Youth and Children's Orchestras of Venezuela, El Sistema was created in 1975 by José Antonio Abreu. Abreu was an economist, musician, and political activist who believed that music should be recognized as a powerful means of social development because it fosters solidarity, harmony, and mutual compassion. Abreu was convinced that music could "unite an entire community." His vision was nothing short of utopian: to create youth orchestras in a population that was impoverished and mostly illiterate.

Born out of the simple, urgent need to get children off the streets, the program began in a garage with eleven children playing on borrowed instruments. (There were no computers involved.) Before long, El Sistema had blossomed into a musical miracle, with more than four hundred learning centers in Venezuela, serving more than 700,000 students. The program now has been replicated in many other countries, including the United States and France. The long-term effect on these children's lives has been analyzed scientifically, and the results are consistent with the science I have cited throughout this book. But the El Sistema project has provided a unique opportunity for analysis of the effect of music on children because this is the first time a study has been done on such a large group of children, and from a developing country. The results are compelling:

- The children who participate in the El Sistema program stay in school longer and pursue higher education more consistently than those who do not.
- The children who participate in the program demonstrate better self-control and less violent behavior. Poignantly,

the biggest changes in behavior are seen in children coming from the most vulnerable and violent domestic situations.

When I think of the children in the El Sistema orchestras, I can't help but remember my own orchestral experience as a child, a teenager, and an adult. At any age, playing in an orchestra is equally demanding and exhilarating. Even if they are all led by a conductor, each individual musician must continuously make micro-adjustments in pitch and tempo and volume to ensure that the music presents as a unified whole. If you have ever watched an orchestral performance, you have seen the constant beautiful swaying of the players. The shared rhythmic pulsation is palpable; the players' bodies appear to be extensions of their instruments.

This is genuine collaboration, transforming those little black dots on the page into something universally beautiful. If a single member of the orchestra does not fully contribute, the whole is compromised. When there are no musical scores, players rely on the aural expertise that their musical enculturation naturally provides. They improvise, take turns, adjust, and listen intently — an experience every bit as challenging and formative as the classical equivalent.

The orchestra is an attractive and entirely plausible model for a peaceful society. In music, as in the rest of life, we don't always play in perfect harmony. But we can learn to work together to overcome our differences and create beauty through unity.

No one can say with certitude exactly what the future is going to look like. There is, however, a consensus among historians, philosophers, scientists, and education specialists: the course of human society will be determined by the existence of moral and ethical parameters surrounding the use of technology, whether it's artificial intelligence, genetic engineering, energy production, or some other seismic innovation as yet unimagined. Our ability to create these parameters will be determined by our capacity to cooperate and to stay close to our collective cultural heritage. I hope you will agree by now that music can help us meet this challenge — and, just maybe, master it.

Whether or not your child wants to become a professional musician is of no importance; practicing music is a lesson in patience, in connecting the dots, in self-determination, in collaboration, and in understanding the function and value of every individual within the societal whole. Music helps us communicate and create together, even when we don't speak the same language or understand one another's cultural codes.

Music builds bridges instead of walls. It can contribute to more happiness and social cohesion in the coming years. Joint musical practice contributes to our sense of belonging. This sense of belonging begins on day one, with the first musical duet between a baby and her parents. Musicking in early childhood reinforces these feelings of security, empathy, and cooperation. We need to bring back simple, natural, and joyful joint musical practice in our homes and schools. This is how we will prepare our children to take their places in the Orchestra of Humankind.

Acknowledgments

This is my first book, and therefore my first attempt at the exercise of permanent public acknowledgment. Quite the challenge: How can any of us acknowledge all of the people who have given their love, advice, and expertise, or provided inspiration? Am I allowed to thank Johannes Brahms, Paul Simon, Marylin Robinson, Muhammad Yunes, Rainer Maria Rilke, Martin Luther King Jr., Joni Mitchell, and Yuval Noah Harari? There is a slight glitch; some are no longer with us, and I don't know the others personally. Yet I'm sure I'm not alone in feeling that their artistic and intellectual output has made the world a better place; I know it has made me a better person.

My father made a straightforward deal with me very early on. The message was "You can achieve *anything* if you work hard enough." I often thought about him while writing this book because it was arduous! Thank you, Mom, for singing to me as a baby, buying that piano, and later going to extravagant lengths to find me wonderful teachers. Libby Van Cleve is "my best friend from all of life," a phrase she coined one day while introducing me to one of her *new* friends. Our friendship began in music more than fifty years ago. Thank you, Libby, for your advice, proofreading, and laughter throughout this new adventure. I want to thank my first musical partners, Brian Ganz and Thomas Otten and their families, for unconditional support and for those endless hours spent rehearsing in your living rooms. The only problem is that these two extraordinary pianists set the standard of musical collaboration very high when we were only teenagers! Janice Girracco and Michael Clancey provide unconditional love, support, enthusiasm, and glorious dinner parties that have pulled me (and others) through many a moment of doubt. And, Janice, you were right when you said, "I read somewhere that you can do something with music and QR codes . . ."

Thank you, mighty and modest Michael Frank, for pinpointing potholes along the way and giving expert advice about the world of writing and publishing books. Joanne Schlesinger, I hereby confer upon you the Nobel Prize for enthusiasm and moral support! Thank you, Sara Gibson, for your belief in the change that this work could bring about, and not just for the happy few. Virginia Isbell, thank you for continually broadening my horizons with your insatiable curiosity and for being there for the meltdowns. Thank you, Mutena Sezgin, for your help and advice on artistic matters. Herbie Hancock, thank you for being the example of a life spent in music and risk taking. I want to be like you when I grow up! Merci, Carène Souhy, pour nos fous rires, nos découvertes, ta joie de vivre, et ton soutien.

The École Koenig community is a beautiful, *very* extended family. It is impossible to adequately thank each of you for your confidence, support, talent, and contribution to this extraordinary adventure. Betsy Schlesinger was the first musician I hired in 1986. Thank you, Betsy, for your talent, your standard of excellence, and for these many years together. Muriel Ossena joined us in 2003. She has ensured the significant growth and transformation we have undergone with grace, clarity, and courage. I could not have written this book without the constant support of these stellar collaborators. I am delighted to be handing over our preschools' day-to-day direction to the multitalented Alix Ferrandon. Thank you, Alix, for making it possible for me to finish this book. I know the children are flourishing on your watch. What an incredible team of strong visionary women — thank you, ladies! Thank you to all the families who have participated in this project and my initial parent readers: Fred Stoltzfus, Magda Schmidt, Victoire Guyot, Sarah and Pierre-Louis Lacoste, and Michelle Minc.

I had many inspiring teachers as a young child, but I may have become a musician because of my early orchestral playing experience. Thank you, Frances Walton, for creating the extraordinary youth symphony programs of the greater Seattle area and for being such an inspiring musician and woman. When my family moved to Washington, DC, pianists Bella Hatfield and Ylda Novik pulled me up by my bootstraps. My first professional flute teacher was Lois Wynn of northern Virginia. I'll never forget when I came for a lesson after not having touched my flute for almost a week. I thought I deserved a break because I had just won a competition. Ms. Wynn disagreed and made this very clear; lesson learned. When I was sixteen, she threw me out of the nest, sending me to study with William Montgomery at the University of Maryland. Dr. Montgomery carefully guided me through the tricky waters of auditions and competitions, and, finally, the choice of "what next?" The Juilliard School was next, with an inspiring faculty, including my flute teacher Paula Robison. I am grateful to have studied in that big cement square at Lincoln Center on Manhattan's Upper West Side — where music, dance, and theater were our oxygen and our raison d'être.

Thank you, Clare Shine, former vice president, and chief program director of the Salzburg Global Seminar; this book was conceived in the elegant Schloss Leopoldskron during the conference "The Neuroscience of Art" you organized. Your faith in music, art, international cooperation, and progress is an inspiration. Salzburg is where I met Anna Abraham, Harry Ballan, and Nigel Osborn, who inspire me daily with their dedication to science, music, creativity, and human resilience.

When I began thinking about this book, my son told me that I should reach out to a *real* writer (unlike me), and preferably a successful one. I took his advice and sent my book proposal to Pamela Druckerman, author of *French Children Don't Throw Food*. Pamela told me that the subject was compelling, but that I had absolutely no idea how to write a book proposal. She directed me toward her former editor Jane Fransson. Thank you for your never flagging enthusiasm and hand holding, Janie; you taught me how to write. Zoë Pagnamenta phoned me the day after the book proposal arrived on her desk. I stepped out of my office to take her call, and when I came back in, I told my colleagues, "I'm not sure, but I think this woman just offered me a contract." Thank you, Zoë, for believing in the book. Zoë sent out the proposal and set up phone meetings for me with interested publishing houses; it was a very long week. Alexander Littlefield from HMH was the last call of the day, and it was Friday. After the call I remember thinking, I hope HMH bids for the book because this guy *really* gets it. Thank you, Alex, for your editorial talent, your continued dedication to this book, and for putting up with a first-time writer.

David Sobel helped me through the last stages of organizing and editing. Although he never expressed this overtly, I think he was deeply concerned about my nonlinear brain and how this was going to go. His wit and humor saved us both! Thank you to the entire team at Houghton Mifflin Harcourt — it has been an honor to work with you.

As always, thank you to every child I have had the joy of seeing grow and thrive in music.

Appendix

MUSICAL SCORES

SCAN ME

I Am a Windmill

by Joan Koenig

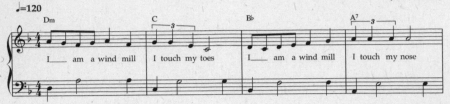

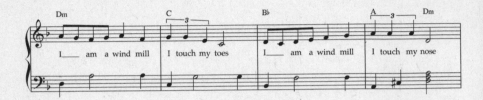

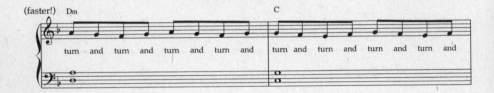

Shake and Stop !

by Joan Koenig

2

I'm gon na shake shake shake two feet in the air   shake shake shake two

feet in the air   I'm gon na shake shake shake two

feet in the air   shake shake shake two   feet in the air

Papageno - Papagena duet
from: *The Magic Flute*

W. A. Mozart
Arr: Joan Koenig

Allegro

Musical Commands

In a Circle

by Joan Koenig & Aurélien Parent

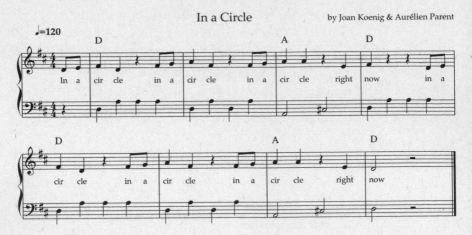

Sit Down

Stand Up

The Life and Times of William Shakespeare

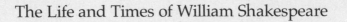

William's Theme

By Joan Koenig

To Be or Not to Be

by Joan Koenig

Parting Is Such Sweet Sorrow

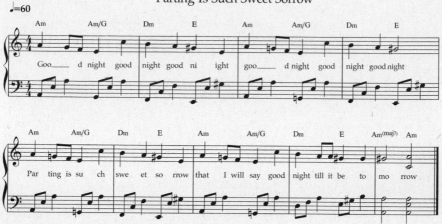

Nian le Dragon

Joan Koenig

L'Ecole Koenig's Phonic Alphabet Song

by Joan Koenig & Aurélien Parent

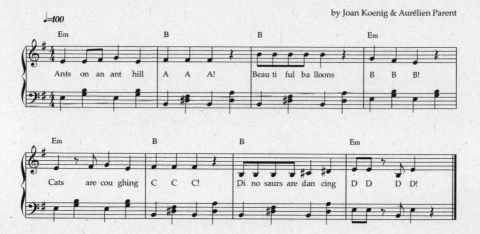

Skip Counting Rap

by Joan Koenig & Aurélien Parent

Notes

1. YEAR ONE

page

5   *means of communication:* Samuel A. Mehr and Max M. Krasnow, "Parent-Offspring Conflict and the Evolution of Infant-Directed Song," *Evolution and Human Behavior* 38, no. 5 (September 2017): 674–84.

7   *Research dating from as far back:* A. J. DeCasper and W. P. Fifer, "Of Human Bonding: Newborns Prefer Their Mothers' Voices," *Science* 208, no. 4448 (June 1980): 1174–76.

8   *babies prefer music to speech:* Sandra Trehub and Takayuki Nakata, "Infants' Responsiveness to Maternal Speech and Singing," Elsevier online, December 2004.

10 *absorbing the codes of her culture:* Emese Nagy and Peter Molnar, "Homo Imitans o Homo Provocans? Human Imprinting Model of Neonatal Imitation," Elsevier online, February 2004.

    forty-two minutes after birth: Andrew N. Meltzoff and M. Keith Moore, "Imitation in Newborn Infants: Exploring the Range of Gestures Imitated and the Underlying Mechanisms," *Developmental Psychology* (November 25, 1989): 954–62.

    what linguists call a "proto-conversation": Maya Pines, "Jerome Bruner Maintains —," *New York Times,* November 29, 1970, https://www.nytimes.com/1970/11/29/archives/jerome-bruner -maintains-infants-are-smarter-than-anybody-thinks.html?smid= em-share.

11 *"Plus or Minus Two":* George A. Miller, "The Magical Number Seven, Plus or Minus Two: Some Limits on Our Capacity for Pro-

cessing Information," *Psychological Review* 63, no. 2 (1956): 81–97, https://doi.org/10.1037/h0043158.

constantly reinventing himself: Pines, "Jerome Bruner Maintains —."

12   *taking the lead:* Colwyn Trevarthen, "The Musical Art of Infant Conversation: Narrating in the Time of Sympathetic Experience, Without Rational Interpretation, Without Words," *Musicae Scientiae* (March 1, 2008): 15–46.

language acquisition support system (LASS): David Bakhurst and Stuart G. Shanker, *Jerome Bruner: Language, Culture, Self* (London: Sage Publications, 2001).

"turn-taking structure of conversation": Colwyn Trevarthen, "Communication and Cooperation in Early Infancy: A Description of Primary Intersubjectivity," in *Before Speech: The Beginning of Interpersonal Communication,* ed. Margaret Bullowa (Cambridge: Cambridge University Press, 1979), 321–47.

He called it child-directed speech: Jerome Bruner, *Child's Talk: Learning to Use Language* (Oxford: Oxford University Press 1983).

13   *a 1975 doctoral dissertation:* Elissa Newport, "Motherese: The Speech of Mothers to Young Children" (PhD diss., University of Pennsylvania, 1975).

an article in the New York Times Magazine: Motherese [Elissa Newport], "On Language; Motherese," *New York Times Magazine,* May 8, 1994, https://www.nytimes.com/1994/05/08/magazine/on-language-motherese.html.

survival of both child and *parent:* Dean Falk, "Prelinguistic Revolution in Early Hominins: Whence Motherese?," *Behavioral and Brain Sciences* 27, no. 4 (2004): 491–503.

How did Motherese develop?: Shelia M. Kennison, *Introduction to Language Development* (Los Angeles: Sage Publications, 2014).

15   *preference for song over speech:* Samuel A. Mehr et al., "Universality and Diversity in Human Song," 366, no. 6468 (November 22, 2019), doi: 10.1126/science.aax0868.

intervened in an orphanage in Bucharest: Fraser Brown and Sophie Webb, "Children Without Play: A Research Project," *Journal of Education,* no. 35 (2005): 139–58.

the "still face" experiment: Dr. Edward Tronick, "Still Face Experiment," November 30, 2009, https://www.youtube.com/watch?v=apzXGEbZht0.

16   *"representations about themselves":* Edward Tronick and Marjorie Beeghly, "Infants' Meaning-Making and the Development of Mental Health Problems," *American Psychologist* 66, no. 2 (February–March 2011): 107–19.

18   *infant musicality and communication:* Stephen Malloch and Colwyn Trevarthen, *Communicative Musicality: Exploring the Basis of Human Companionship* (Oxford: Oxford University Press, 2010).

20   *more than twenty years of research:* A. J. Blood et al., "Emotional Responses to Pleasant and Unpleasant Music Correlate with Limbic Brain Regions," *Nature Neuroscience* 2 (1999): 382–87.

22   *research indicates it is the* quality: Roberta Michnick Golinkoff et al., "(Baby) Talk to Me: The Social Context of Infant-Directed Speech and Early Language Acquisition," SAGEpub.com, 2015.

2. YEAR TWO

29   *musical practice all over the world:* Mehr et al., "Universality and Diversity in Human Song."

30   *very early in life:* Celia A. Brownwell, "Early Development of Prosocial Behavior: Current Perspectives," *Infancy* 18, no. 1 (January–February 2013): 1–9.

     never seen a conductor: Trevarthen, "The Musical Art of Infant Conversation."

     specific areas of the brain: Marcel Zentner and Tuomas Eerola, "Rhythmic Engagement with Music in Infancy," *Proceedings of the National Academy of Sciences of the United States* 107, no. 13 (March 30, 2010): 5771, www.pnas.org/cgi/doi/10.1073/pnas.1000121107.

31   *development of this vital system:* Valerie Strauss, "Let's Face It, Keeping Children Sedentary for Most of Their Waking Hours Is Causing Harm," *Washington Post,* November 11, 2016, https://www.washingtonpost.com/news/answer-sheet/wp/2016/11/11/lets-face-it-keeping-children-sedentary-for-most-of-their-waking-hours-is-causing-harm/.

     guiding our bodies from dawn to dusk: Sarah Kahn and Robert Chang, "Anatomy of the Vestibular System: A Review," *NeuroRehabilitation* 32, no. 3 (2013): 437–43.

32   *parked too often in front of screens:* Amy and Evelyn Guttman, "What Screen Time and Screen Media Do to Your Child's Brain and

Sensory Processing Ability," *Hands On OT*, March 28, 2017, https://handsonotrehab.com/screen-time-brain-sensory-processing/.

control of posture and mobility: Carla Hannaford, *Smart Moves: Why Learning Is Not All in Your Head* (Salt Lake City: Great River Books, 1995).

according to a recent study: Isabelle Peretz and Dominique T. Vuvan, "Prevalence of Congenital Amusia," *European Journal of Human Genetics* 25, no. 2 (February 22, 2017): 1–6.

33 *first things infants respond to:* W. Tecumseh Fitch, "Four Principles of Bio-musicology.nous, "Philosophical Transactions of the Royal Society (2015), http://dx.doi.org/10.1098/rstb.2014.0091.

especially when music is involved: Dana Lavalley, "Incorporating Sensory Input into Music Therapy Sessions," *Therabeat*, September 21, 2017, http://www.therabeat.com/news-and-events/2017/9/21/incorporating-sensory-input-into-music-therapy-sessions.

indicators of insufficient vestibular development: "The Vestibular System — Sensory Processing Disorder," Occupational Therapy Helping Children, https://occupationaltherapy.com.au/about-us/.

34 *"learning difficulties and dyslexia are rare":* Hannaford, *Smart Moves*, xxv.

39 *as well as her physical confidence:* Rose Marie Rine, "Vestibular Rehabilitation for Children," *Seminars in Hearing* 39 (August 2018): 334–44.

42 *during this preverbal period:* T. Christina Zhao and Patricia K. Kuhl, "Musical Intervention Enhances Infants' Neural Processing of Temporal Structure in Music and Speech," *Proceedings of the National Academy of Sciences of the United States* 113, no. 19 (May 11, 2016): 5212–17.

or, more simply, babbling: D. Kimbrough Oller et al., "Preterm and Full Term Infant Vocalization and the Origin of Language," *Scientific Reports*, October 14, 2019.

45 Music, Language, and the Brain: Aniruddh D. Patel, *Music, Language, and the Brain* (New York: Oxford University Press, 2009).

the OPERA hypothesis: Aniruddh D. Patel, "Why Would Musical Training Benefit the Neural Encoding of Speech? The OPERA Hypothesis," *Frontiers in Psychology*, June 29, 2011.

46 *"Phoneme Symphony":* Sigrun Lang et al., "Canonical Babbling: A

Marker for Earlier Identification of Late Detected Developmental Disorders?" *Current Developmental Disorders Reports* 6, no. 3 (May 30, 2019): 111–18.

49 *a child's future linguistic development:* Patricia K. Kuhl, Feng-Ming Tsao, and Huei-Mei Liu, "Speech Perception in Infancy Predicts Language Development in the Second Year of Life: A Longitudinal Study," *Child Development* 75, no. 4 (July–August 2004): 1067–84.
she could find out: Patricia Kuhl, "The Neurogenetics of Language," September 6, 2015, Leaders in Pharmaceutical Innovation, series E. 2, https://pharmaceuticalintelligence.com/2015/09/06/the-neurogenetics-of-language-patricia-kuhl/.
twelve short Mandarin Chinese "lessons": Patricia K. Kuhl, Feng-Ming Tsao, and Huei-Mei Liu, "Foreign-Language Experience in Infancy: Effects of Short-Term Exposure and Social Interaction on Phonetic Learning," *Proceedings of the National Academy of Sciences of the United States* 100, no. 15 (July 22, 2003): 9096–9101.

50 *many in circulation:* Sanne Dekker et al., "Neuromyths in Education: Prevalence and Predictors of Misconceptions Among Teachers," *Frontiers in Psychology* 3, no. 429 (October 18, 2012): 429.
study in the British scientific journal Nature: Frances H. Rauscher, Gordon L. Shaw, and Catherine N. Ky, "Music and Spatial Task Performance," *Nature* 365, no. 611 (October 14, 1993).

51 *the very same journal,* Nature: Christopher Chabris, "Prelude or Requiem for the 'Mozart Effect'?," Nature 400 (August 1999): 826–27, https://doi.org/10.1038/23608.
"Mozart Effect — Schmozart Effect: Jakob Pietschnig, Martin Voracek, and Anton K. Formann, "Mozart Effect — Shmozart Effect: A Meta-Analysis," *Intelligence* 38 (May–June 2010): 314–23.
generating a lot of confusion: Samuel A. Mehr, "Miscommunication of Science: Music Cognition Research in the Popular Press," *Frontiers in Psychology,* July 20, 2015, https://doi.org/10.3389/fpsyg.2015.00988.

3. YEAR THREE

59 *"the linguistic genius of babies":* Patricia Kuhl, "The Linguistic Genius of Babies," TEDxRainier, 2010, youtube.com/watch?v=G2XBlkHW954.

61 *our need for pleasure and reward:* Robert J. Zatorre and Valorie
N. Salimpoor, "From Perception to Pleasure: Music and Its Neural
Substrates," *Proceedings of the National Academy of Sciences of the
United States* 110 (June 18, 2013): 10430–37.
feel so very good: Robert J. Zatorre and Valorie N. Salimpoor,
"Why Music Makes Our Brain Sing," *New York Times,* June 7, 2013,
https://www.nytimes.com/2013/06/09/opinion/sunday/why-music
-makes-our-brain-sing.html.

68 *by his expert older siblings:* Victor Wooten, "Music As a Language,"
TEDxGabriola Island, 2013, https://youtu.be/2zvjW9arAZ0.

70 *even more important than IQ:* Angela L. Duckworth and Martin
E. P. Seligman, "Self-Discipline Outdoes IQ in Predicting Academic
Performance of Adolescents," *Psychological Science* (December
2005): 939–44.

74 *emotional states as well as age:* Hamish G. MacDougall and Steven
T. Moore, "Marching to the Beat of the Same Drummer: The Spontaneous Tempo of Human Locomotion," *Journal of Applied Physiol-
ogy* 99 (September 2005): 1164–73.

75 *potential for empathy and cooperation:* Tal-Chen Rabinowitch and
Andrew N. Meltzoff, "Synchronized Movement Experience En-
hances Peer Cooperation in Preschool Children," Elsevier online,
August 2017.
experiment with groups of four-year-olds: Michael Tomasello and
Sebastian Kirschner, "Joint Music Making Promotes Prosocial Be-
havior in 4-Year-Old Children," *Evolution and Human Behavior* 31
(September 2010): 354–64.

76 *effect of rhythmic entrainment in babies:* Laura K. Cirelli, Stepha-
nie J. Wan, and Laurel J. Trainor, "Social Effects of Movement Synchrony: Increased Infant Helpfulness Only Transfers to Affiliates of
Synchronously Moving Partners," *Infancy* (March 7, 2016): 1–15.

77 *with no conscious effort:* Michael H. Thaut et al., "Neurobiological
Foundations of Neurologic Music Therapy: Rhythmic Entrainment
and the Motor System," *Frontiers in Psychology,* February 18, 2015,
doi: 10.3389/fpsyg.2014.01185.

80 *working in New York in the 1960s:* Frances Webber Aronoff, *Music
and Young Children* (New York: Holt Rinehart and Winston, 1971).

81 *or any other skill:* Samual Mehr et al., "Two Randomized Trials

Provide No Consistent Evidence for Nonmusical Cognitive Benefits of Brief Preschool Music Enrichment," *PLOS One* (December 11,
2013).

84 *"there has to be a you":* Martin Buber, *I-Thou* (Edinburgh: T&T
Clark, 1937).

or benefits, of musical engagement: Stefan Koelsch, "From Social
Contact to Social Cohesion — The 7 Cs," *Music and Medicine* 5, no.
4 (October 2013): 204–9.

4. YEAR FOUR

87 *Days of Miracle and Wonder:* Paul Simon, "The Boy in the Bubble,"
Graceland (Warner Bros., 1986).

89 *help people negotiate exponential change:* Simon Whittemore,
"Transversal Competencies Essential for Proofing the Future Work-
force," ResearchGate, October 2018.

91 *still considered groundbreaking:* George Lakoff and Mark Johnson,
Metaphors We Live By (Chicago: University of Chicago Press, 1980).

100 *"sound without any reference point":* Diana Deutsch, *The Psychology of Music* (Cambridge: Academic Press, 2012).

102 *a sign of intelligence:* Alex Stone, "Is Your Child Lying to
You? That's Good," *New York Times,* January 5, 2018, https://
www.nytimes.com/2018/01/05/opinion/sunday/children-lying
-intelligence.html?auth=login-facebook.

"distinct from those of others": Baris Korkmaz, "Theory of Mind and
Neurodevelopmental Disorders of Childhood," *Pediatric Research*
69, no. 5 (2011).

104 *weak rhythm skills:* Enik Ladányi et al., "Is Atypical Rhythm a
Risk Factor for Developmental Speech and Language Disorders?,"
WIREs Cognitive Science, April 2020, https://doi.org/10.1002/wcs
.1528.

110 *signs of deeper challenges:* Ladányi et al., "Is Atypical Rhythm a
Risk Factor for Developmental Speech and Language Disorders?"
dyslexia, ASD, and ADHD: Jessica L. Slater and Matthew C.
Tate, "Timing Deficits in ADHD: Insights from the Neuroscience of
Musical Rhythm," *Frontiers in Computational Neuroscience* (July 6,
2018).

111 *rhythms and cues of spoken language:* Usha Goswami et al.,

"Amplitude Envelope Onsets and Developmental Dyslexia: A New Hypothesis," *Proceedings of the National Academy of Sciences of the United States* 99, no. 16 (August 6, 2002): 10911–16.

113 *we've had spoken language:* Vyv Evans, "How Old Is Language? On Time Machines, Talking Neanderthals, and the Long(ish) Past of Language," *Psychology Today*, February 19, 2015, https://www.psychologytoday.com/intl/blog/language-in-the-mind/201502/how-old-is-language?destination=node/1071350.

114 *study run at the University of Cambridge:* Goswami et al., "Amplitude Envelope Onsets and Developmental Dyslexia," lxiv.
overcoming these difficulties: Michel Habib et al., "Music and Dyslexia: A New Musical Training Method to Improve Reading and Related Disorders," PubMed.gov, January 22, 2016.

115 *playwright Thomas d'Urfey in 1698:* Thomas d'Urfey, *The Campaigners* (1698), http://nurseryrhymesmg.com/rhymes/pat_a_cake.htm.
fairy-tale master Charles Perrault: https://www.pookpress.co.uk/project/mother-goose-rhymes-history/.
thinly disguised horror stories: Jennifer M. Wood, "The Dark Origins of 11 Classic Nursery Rhymes," Mental Floss.com, October 28, 2015, https://www.mentalfloss.com/article/55035/dark-origins-11-classic-nursery-rhymes.

5. YEAR FIVE

126 *autonomy, creativity, and happiness:* Pasi Sahlberg and William Doyle, "To Really Learn, Our Children Need the Power of Play," *Wall Street Journal*, August 8, 2019.
can influence a child's development: Sandra W. Russ, Andrew L. Robins, and Beth A. Christiano, "Pretend Play: Longitudinal Prediction of Creativity and Affect in Fantasy in Children," *Creativity Research Journal* (June 8, 2010): 129–39.

129 *thirty years of data:* Michael D. Chandler, "Improvisation in Elementary General Music: A Review of the Literature," SAGEpub.com, March 16, 2018.

135 *through creative experimentation:* Christopher D. Azzara, "Audiation-Based Improvisation Techniques and Elementary Instrumental Students' Music Achievement," *Journal of Research in Music Education* 41, no. 4 (1993): 328–42.

by their first birthday: Erin E. Hannon and Sandra E. Trehub, "Tuning In to Musical Rhythms: Infants Learn More Readily Than Adults," *Proceedings of the National Academy of Sciences of the United States* 102, no. 35 (August 30, 2005): 12639–43.

We call it "going home": Susan Young, "The Interpersonal Dimension: A Potential Source of Musical Creativity for Young Children?," *Musicae Scientiae* 7, no. 1, suppl. (2003): 175–91, doi: 10.1177/10298649040070S109.

145 *The seven-note scale:* Steven Brown and Joseph Jordania, "Universals in the World's Musics," *Psychology of Music* 41, no. 2 (March 2011): 229–48.

149 *"the day of his first music lesson":* Wooten, "Music As a Language."

150 *the interval of a perfect fifth:* https://www.phys.uconn.edu/~gibson/Notes/Section3_2/Sec3_2.htm.

their descriptive names in ancient Greece: The New Grove Dictionary of Music and Musicians (London: Macmillan, 2001).

one octave (eight notes) higher: https://www.phys.uconn.edu/~gibson/Notes/Section3_3/Sec3_3.htm.

153 *paradoxically a musical universal:* Mehr et al., "Universality and Diversity in Human Song."

156 *developmental psychologist Lev Vygotsky:* Alex Kozulin et al., eds., *Vygotsky's Educational Theory in Cultural Context* (Cambridge: Cambridge University Press, 2003).

157 *our families, and our communities:* Salhberg and Doyle, "To Really Learn, Our Children Need the Power of Play."

158 *the academy's 2018 clinical report:* Michael Yogman et al., "The Power of Play: A Pediatric Role in Enhancing Development in Young Children," *Pediatrics* (September 2018).

160 *and a fifty-year follow-up:* Bonnie Cramond et al., "A Report on the 40-Year Follow-Up of the Torrance Tests of Creative Thinking: Alive and Well in the New Millennium," *Gifted Child Quarterly* (October 1, 2005).

161 *Torrance's data were analyzed yet again:* James C. Kaufman, Jonathan A. Plucker, and Christina M. Russell, "Identifying and Assessing Creativity As a Component of Giftedness," *Journal of Psychoeducational Assessment* (December 5, 2011).

An alarming study was conducted: Kyung Hee Kim, "The Creativity Crisis: The Decrease in Creative Thinking Scores on the Torrance Tests of Creative Thinking," *Creativity Research Journal* (November 9, 2011): 285–95.

"People prefer to learn creatively": E. Paul Torrance and H. Tammy Safter, *The Incubation Model of Teaching: Getting Beyond the Aha!* (Buffalo, NY: Bearly, June 1990).

162 *"social units in powerful ways":* Richard Ashley, "Musical Improvisation," in *Oxford Handbook of Music Psychology,* 2nd ed. (New York: Oxford University Press, 2016), 667–79.

6. YEAR SIX

171 *extremely advanced pitch recognition:* Diana Deutsch and Kevin Dooley, "Absolute Pitch among Students in an American Music Conservatory: Association with Tone Language Fluency," *Journal of the Acoustical Society of America* 125, no. 4 (May 2009): 2683.

second-language acquisition: Bastien Intartaglia et al., "Music Training Enhances the Automatic Neural Processing of Foreign Speech Sounds," *Scientific Reports* 7, no. 1 (October 3, 2017).

172 *what scientists call "culture-bound":* Kuhl, "The Linguistic Genius of Babies."

174 *age at which the song is learned:* Lutz Jäncke, "Music, Memory and Emotion," *Journal of Biology* (August 8, 2008).

175 *located it in the human heart:* David Bloch, "Aristotle on Memory and Recollection," Brill.com, August 31, 2007.

paths and divisions of memory types: R. C. Atkinson and R. M. Shiffrin, "Human Memory: A Proposed System and Its Control Processes," *Psychology of Learning and Motivation* 2 (1968): 89–195.

176 *emotions in the memory process:* Jäncke, "Music, Memory, and Emotion."

both implicit and explicit memory centers: Marc Ettlinger, Elizabeth H. Margulis, and Patrick C. M. Wong, "Implicit Memory in Music and Language," *Frontiers in Psychology* (September 9, 2011).

177 *"Not everybody agrees":* Robert Zatorre, e-mail to the author, August 19, 2019.

179 *memory instantly to the surface:* Heidi Mitchell, "Why Does Music Aid in Memorization? A Memory Expert on How Songs Get Stuck in Your Mind," *Wall Street Journal,* December 30, 2013, https://

www.wsj.com/articles/SB100014240527023044838045792846 8
2214451364.

180 *One of the most poignant examples:* "Meet the Hero — Douglas
Hegdahl," Lowell Milken Center for Unsung Heroes, 2020, https://
www.lowellmilkencenter.org/programs/projects/view/douglas
-hegdahl-the-incredibly-stupid-one/hero.

182 *before we become aware of the learning:* Ettlinger, Margulis, and
Wong, "Implicit Memory in Music and Language."

184 *published in 2000:* "Teaching Children to Read: An Evidence
Based Assessment of the Scientific Research Literature on Reading and Its Implications for Reading Instruction," National Reading Panel, 2000, https://www.nichd.nih.gov/sites/default/files/
publications/pubs/nrp/Documents/report.pdf.
mandatory training for teachers: Emily Hanford, "Hard Words —
Why Aren't Kids Being Taught to Read?," APM Reports, September
2018, https://www.apmreports.org/episode/2018/09/10/hard-words
-why-american-kids-arent-being-taught-to-read.

185 *likelihood of deep and permanent learning:* Michelle M. Tomlinson,
"Literacy and Music in Early Childhood: Multimodal Learning and
Design," SAGEpub.com, September 4, 2013.

191 *transfer to other areas:* Samuel Mehr, "Music and Success," *New
York Times,* December 20, 2013, https://www.nytimes.com/2013/12/
22/opinion/sunday/music-and-success.html.

CONCLUSION

197 *from one field to another:* The discussion that follows draws from
Andreas Schleicher, *World Class: How to Build a 21st-Century
School System* (Paris: OECD, May 29, 2018).

198 *notions of* rising up *and* flow: *The Online Etymology Dictionary,*
https://www.etymonline.com/word/orchestra.

199 *pursue higher education more consistently:* Nina Kraus et al., "Music Enrichment Programs Improve the Neural Encoding of Speech
in At-Risk Children," *Journal of Neuroscience* (September 3, 2014).

200 *vulnerable and violent domestic situations:* Xiomara Alemán et al.,
"The Effects of Musical Training on Child Development: A Randomized Trial of El Sistema in Venezuela," *Prevention Science* (November 2016).

Index